ENTERTAINING WITH

THE SOPRANOS^{SM}

As compiled by
CARMELA SOPRANO

Written by Allen Rucker

•

Recipes by Michele Scicolone

•

Series created by David Chase

HBO®
IT'S NOT TV. IT'S HBO.™

WARNER BOOKS

NEW YORK   BOSTON

Warner Books

Time Warner Book Group
1271 Avenue of the Americas, New York, NY 10020
Visit our Web site at www.twbookmark.com.

Printed in the United States of America

First Edition: February 2006
10 9 8 7 6 5 4 3 2 1

Library of Congress Cataloging-in-Publication Data

Rucker, Allen.
    Entertaining with the Sopranos : compiled by Carmela Soprano / written by Allen Rucker ; recipes by Michele Scicolone ; series created by David Chase.–1st ed.
        p. cm.
    Includes index.
    ISBN-13: 978-0-446-57911-7
    ISBN-10: 0-446-57911-4
1. Entertaining. 2. Cookery, Italian. 3. Parties. 4. *Sopranos* (Television program)
I. Scicolone, Michele. II. Title.
    TX731.R83 2006
    642'.4-dc22   2005023619

Interior designed by Mada Design, Inc.
Front cover photograph by Barry Wetcher/HBO
Front cover photo, Costume Designer: Juliet Polcsa
Front cover photo, Hair: Anthony Veader
Front cover photo, Makeup: Kymbra Callaghan Kelley
Back cover cast photograph by Abbot Genser/HBO
Endpapers photos by Abbot Genser/HBO

Interior photo credits:
i, 6, 9 (bottom), 24, 26, 44 (bottom), 93, 110 (top and bottom), 167 (top) Anthony Neste/HBO

1, 15, 17, 23, 25, 31, 36, 37, 39, 41, 49, 55, 59, 61, 63, 71, 81, 85, 91, 99, 105, 107, 113, 117, 119, 129, 133, 135, 143, 147, 149, 159, 163, 165, 175, 177, 181, 183, 191, 197 Ellen Silverman

2 (top), 2 (bottom), 4, 5, 12, 28, 46, 70, 73, 76 (top and bottom), 90, 92, 94 and 95, 108, 134, 136, 148, 152, 164, 168, 169, 170, 182, 186 Abbot Genser/HBO

9 (top), 10, 11, 13, 27, 29, 40, 42, 44 (top), 45, 47, 74, 75, 79 (top and bottom), 96, 97, 106, 109, 137 (left and right), 139, 150, 151, 167 (bottom), 184, 187, 198 Barry Wetcher/HBO

CKNOWLEDGMENTS

My eternal gratitude to David Chase, Ilene Landress, Bree Conover, Richard Oren, Russell Schwartz, and Felicia Lipchik Gell for all of their help and support. Special thanks to Chris Albrecht, Carolyn Strauss, Miranda Heller, Mike Garcia, Victoria Frazier, Tracey Barrett-Lee, Jeff Peters, and all the other people at *The Sopranos* and HBO who make books like this so darn much fun to do. Thanks to food stylist Anne Disrude, prop stylist Betty Alfenito, and Triserve Rental. Michele Scicolone is a joy to work with and an expert on all things Italian-American, life as well as food. Two people deserve enormous credit and acknowledgment: entertaining specialist Kathleen Renda for providing a thousand and one great ideas and editor Natalie Kaire for overseeing every aspect of this enterprise. Super agent Jay Mandel, kudos on the new baby, and, as always, my love to Ann-Marie, Blaine, and Max.

CONTENTS

INTRODUCTION

ello and welcome to our exciting new book on entertaining. While I am not a professional writer, I do feel I am a seasoned party planner and hostess and love entertaining. As time inevitably goes by and my family grows up and scatters with the wind, I've come to love and appreciate family gatherings even more. I feel a special tug in my heart for all those occasions, from wedding receptions to Grandpa's seventieth birthday party, where the only real task is to enjoy each other's company. Thus the impetus for this book on the joys of entertaining—a chance to elaborate on those special events that my children might then be able to pass on to their children to keep the flame of family and friendship alive.

We often take these social rituals for granted, but we do so at our own peril. They are more fragile than we think. Like fine crystal, they break easily and are hard to glue back together.

As we all know, it's so easy to say one Christmas, "Oh, let's just forget the big Christmas Eve celebration this year, order in pizza, and watch *It's a Wonderful Life* on cable." You do that and think it's a one-time-only event, but it's the *next* Christmas when the effects are truly felt. Your grown daughter might say, "Heck, I'm

too tired to go home to eat pizza. I can order pizza here in my place in New York and just call home collect." The ties, in other words, begin to unravel because the tradition has lost both its familiarity and its magic.

Of course that annual Christmas Eve affair shouldn't be a stale rendition of last year. If you repeat the same old routine—same baked ziti, same Aunt Lena's tiramisu, same tinsel balls on the tree—your family and friends will either fall asleep on the couch or park themselves in front of the new flat-screen TV. You can get too stuck in a tradition in the same way you can get unstuck. The best way to keep things fresh and new is to think of each such occasion as the very first one you've ever hosted and mix old and new elements in your own unique fashion. If you have grown children, like we do, you can't force them to live close to home, but when you put your heart in family

gatherings, you can lure them back for moments that will both reassure them of their family's love and remind them that you make the best food on earth!

Let's face it, all families have problems. Parents fight and sometimes separate; kids rebel and sometimes get lost and confused; grandparents drive everyone crazy; and in-laws are often thoughtless or imposing. So, to maintain harmony, there must be occasional time-outs where hatchets get buried, grievances get filed away, and latent bad feelings take a holiday. This book is dedicated to those moments.

As you probably gathered from my name, I am an Italian-American, married to an Italian-American, and raised in the traditions of Italian-Americans. Our forefathers emigrated from Southern Italy, and in my case, also Sicily, and in general we define our roots as Neapolitan, after the city of Naples. My husband has a deep and abiding affection for all things Neapolitan, as do I, so this book naturally reflects the food we love and the customs we cherish. Some of the occasions I write about are "ethnocentric," meaning they pertain specifically to our Italian and Catholic heritage or simply our tried-and-true ways. You may not celebrate a confirmation in your

house or serve a big buffet after a funeral. But we all go through the same life passages—birth, coming of age, marriage, birthdays, and, sadly, death. We all have special occasions. So feel free to take the ideas and recipes here and adapt them to your own rites of passage, whatever they might be. Maybe your idea of "confirmation" is going from the eighth grade to the ninth or passing the driver's test. Maybe "graduation" in your family means successfully

completing boot camp. Just take the suggestions in the chapter on graduations, add a little military spit and polish, and have a great time.

Many of these traditions have stories attached to them and were passed down by word of mouth or sitting at Mama's feet in the kitchen; they date back to a small village in Naples or Avellino, a nearby province where my husband's family is rooted. Other time-honored customs, as I've come to learn, were invented

BAR BASICS
by Arthur Bucco

Food and drink, naturally, are the main ingredients of entertaining. Food will be dealt with on a chapter-by-chapter basis, as will selected beverages, but I thought an overview of at-home "bar basics" would make a good reference right off the top. For this I've called in an expert, restaurateur (Nuovo Vesuvio) Arthur "Artie" Bucco. *CS*

Thank you, Carmela. When serving wine or alcohol at home, remember a few basic rules and you'll never be caught short, i.e., socially embarrassed. You needn't have twelve varieties of single-malt Scotch or an obscure Greek liqueur to handle the drink requirements of an at-home party, large or small. Just push-pin the following guidelines on the pantry wall next to "In Case of Fire."

- If you are expecting more than forty guests and plan to serve mixed drinks, hire a bartender. They run about $30 to 40 an hour. Or if Uncle Bruno considers himself a skilled mixer of drinks, assign him the job. Like grilling on a barbecue, soon others will pitch in with their own specialties.
- Split the bar into two areas—mixed drinks and wines, for instance. If it's a houseful of people, think about prepouring glasses of wine, at least for the first round.
- For the first hour of the party, count on two drinks per person. For each hour after that, one drink per person. These are just averages, of course, but it helps in the planning. A normal bottle of liquor (750 milliliters) will yield about six four-ounce glasses.
- If you are serving wine with dinner, figure one to three glasses per person. One bottle holds about four glasses. So: You'll need two to three bottles for every four people. Then add another bottle for good measure, e.g., in case there are a couple of big drinkers at the table.
- Ice is important, for wine and soft drinks. Estimate one and a half to two pounds of ice per person. Get a chilling tub and fill it with ice; it could take forty to fifty pounds. It takes a good thirty minutes to chill any drink this way. If you need to chill wine fast, get an ice bucket, fill it with ice, ice-cold water, and ¼ cup salt. Then wrap the bottle in wet paper towels and stick it in. Don't ask me how it works, but it does, and knowing how often we are all faced with a warm bottle of wine, you'll be trying this soon.
- Have plenty of glassware. You don't want a guest drinking Scotch from a champagne flute or champagne from a Scotch glass, and you don't want anyone drinking from Styrofoam or plastic. If you don't got 'em, rent 'em. People go through a lot of glasses. Plan on four glasses per guest at a dinner or buffet, less for a cocktail party, depending on what you're serving. In general, don't skimp on glassware or ice. Buy cheap liquor, but at least present it nicely.
- A well-stocked bar offers guests a lot of choices. Your liquor inventory should include the regular suspects: gin, rum, vodka, Scotch, bourbon, tequila, beer, and a variety of wines. Other drink-mixing essentials: sweet and dry vermouth, Cointreau, sour mix, mineral water, and juices—cranberry, orange, and tomato. A jigger is de rigueur and the best kind is a two-ended jigger/pony with one end a 1½-ounce jigger and the other end a 1-ounce pony. Add a cocktail shaker and a cocktail strainer, a pitcher to hold stirred drinks, and a blender for mixing frozen drinks like margaritas. One last thing: a cutting board and a sharp knife for slicing lemons and limes. Oh, yeah, and a handbook on making drinks, so you'll know what you're doing.

in America—but their many admirers swear they came over on the boat with Great-Grandpa Orazio or Great-Grandma Concetta. Such is the love of the past in the Italian-American household. If we can't remember it, we invent it.

Beyond Old World influences, some of the ideas here might not strike you as particularly Italian, and you'd be right. Remember, we are not only *Italian*-Americans, we are also Italian-*Americans*. We live here, just like many of you, and we can't help but be swayed and inspired by many homegrown practices that we enjoy as much as any other American group, from Super Bowl Sunday to a monthly book club luncheon. So we blend old and new, Italiano and Americano, and we hope you enjoy our richly varied entertaining soufflé.

This labor of love is the work of dozens of people, all close family or friends. Credit for the whole idea goes to my husband, Anthony Soprano, who successfully argued that such a commercial venture was a logical extension of my main "job," that of wife, mother, and amateur hostess. Our two wonderful children, Meadow and Anthony, Jr., added their opinions where appropriate, and our large extended family of friends and relatives joyfully contributed when asked. I must also thank all the authors of all those splendid books on entertaining that I devoured before setting forth on this adventure. Without your inspiration, I would have never even gotten through this introduction, let alone a whole book!

So, as we do in our household, I raise a glass of *Southern* Italian wine and say to all, *"Salut'!"* To your health! And, please, enjoy the life you've been given, not to mention the people you've been given to spend it with.

THE PERFECT HOSTESS

Until I read the following news clipping as a young bride, I really didn't understand the art of hostessing. It's been pinned on my kitchen bulletin board ever since. You may want to pin it on yours.

Dear Happy Homemaker: I have never thrown a good party. People just don't have much fun and often leave early. My husband says I'm a loser. What am I doing wrong?
Clueless from Camden

Dear Clueless: I can't make you the perfect hostess overnight, but you have to know the basics. 1. Don't spend all your time in the kitchen. You're a hostess, not a charwoman. 2. For the first half hour, greet each guest at the door. Parties are intimidating to many, so say something nice and effusive to *everyone*. Just fill in the blank: "Hey, ___, we're so glad you could make it! It wouldn't be a party without you, ___!" Practice this a hundred times, using different names. 3. Take their coats and lead them into the party, toward someone they know or the bar. If they don't know anyone, then introduce them to someone and prime the conversation. "Dick here is a stay-at-home accountant. Isn't that interesting?" 4. Work the room. Seriously. Keep circulating the whole night. Cover the whole territory more than once. Your goal is to become a Master Mingler and Small-talker. 5. Give the shy and awkward types a job like passing around appetizers or pouring champagne; they'll make friends among the heavy eaters or drinkers. 6. No matter how much hubby criticizes or belittles you as a hostess, don't get drunk. Rots of ruck, HH.

WHITE VERSUS RED

by Arthur Bucco

Okay, most people don't know what wine to serve with what food, so they buy some bland rosé and hope it doesn't taste like swill water after a mouthful of spaghetti puttanesca. The traditional rule is: white wines go with fish, seafood, and poultry, red wine goes with beef and your game meats. That's better than nothing, but doesn't always hold true, I'm sorry to say. A fruity red wine, say, won't taste great with a sirloin steak. It'll probably taste better with a nice chicken dish, which breaks the rule. So what do you do? Consider Rule #2 and Rule #3.

Rule #2: Match rich, hearty wines with rich, hearty food and match lighter dishes with more delicate, lighter wines. So, if you have steak, a "big" meat dish, think of a "big" red wine like a California Burgundy. I guess you could match it with a big white wine, too, but I don't know of any big white wines.

Rule #3: Figure it out yourself. Sweet foods often go well with drier wines. Spicy foods might play off a more fruity wine. When no guests are around, put a dish on the table with two or three distinctly different kinds of wine and see which tickles your palate. Then you can start your own rule book.

If you're serving a series of wines throughout a meal, serve dry before sweet and light before heavy. Save the sweetest for dessert. For example: start with champagne, follow with a red wine like a Pinot Noir, and end with a French Sauternes (not an American all-purpose Sauterne). Something like that.

Chapter 1

WELCOME TO THE FAMILY:
BAPTISMS, COMMUNIONS, AND CONFIRMATIONS

Life on earth begins at birth and so does the life of treasured family gatherings. There are many ways of welcoming a newborn into the family. A come-see-the-baby open house is a wonderful way to show off a new member of the family. If you were in a birth-training class like Lamaze, for example, invite all the newborns to join the party and take a "class" photo. It doesn't get cuter than a dozen darling babies lined up on your sofa.

Devout Catholics that they were, the first big event in my parents' house after my birth was the baptism. The ceremony was simple—I was brought to the church by my godparents and my mom stayed home to make rice balls. The after-party was even simpler. People crowded into the little all-purpose room in the church basement and ate the potluck offerings brought by family and friends. There was no "menu" per se. Whatever Aunt Teresa or Mrs. Nuncio felt inspired to fix—cold cuts, potato croquettes, eggplant Parmesan, a *'shcarole* salad—was heartily consumed.

My family has kept this infant ritual going, although the menu has certainly changed, and I'm sure your family has your own that is just as meaningful. I will speak of the Catholic way, but again, please modify and generalize in any way you see fit. The sacrament of baptism, for Catholics, is the beginning of a lifelong process of commitment to the church and its teachings. It's a public acknowledgment that you, the parents, plan to raise this child as a Catholic. Other religious traditions, of course, have baptism ceremonies, which may differ in the particulars of word and gesture but are similar in spirit. I'm ashamed to say that I have no idea how, say, Buddhists or Muslims announce the birth of a new child, but even without a specific religious ritual, just the magic of birth itself is a raison d'être for a large family celebration.

There are other milestones of pre-adult life that are a cause for gathering and rejoicing. There is First Holy Communion, which is exactly what it sounds like, a child's first communion in the church, usually occurring around the age of seven or eight. This is a Catholic's first celebration of the Eucharist, the consecrated wafer representing the body and blood of Christ. Seven or eight is considered the "age of reason," when a child can distinguish between ordinary bread and the Eucharist.

At a slightly older age, around the time of adolescence, comes a major event in a young Catholic's life, confirmation. A young person preparing for confirmation spends two years in a program of religious education before he or she re-enters the church as a full-fledged member of the congregation. This is somewhat akin to the Jewish tradition of the bar mitzvah for males or bas mitzvah for females. You reach a certain age, you learn the customs and requirements of the religion, and you become a man or woman. It's a natural stepping stone to adulthood.

The confirmation party for our son, Anthony, Jr., or AJ, was a special day. He was thirteen at the time, a customary age for confirmation these days. Like many young people in our "do-what-feels-good" consumer culture, AJ was seriously questioning the existence of God and the meaning of life as he prepared for entry into the church. His now dearly departed grandmother, unhappy in her old age, had apparently told him that life was "a big nothing" and that "you die in your own arms." My husband, thank God, intervened and AJ quickly regained his faith. A few words of wisdom from his godfather, Salvatore Bonpensiero, also did a world of good.

What is a "godfather," you might be asking? We've all heard the word used in various ways,

NOTES ON AN INVITATION

Anthony and Carmela Soprano
Announce the Confirmation of their son,

Anthony Soprano, Jr.

St. Peter and Paul's Catholic Church
West Orange, N.J.

Father Philip Intintola presiding

Saturday, the fourth of October
At one o'clock in the afternoon

A baptism or confirmation usually calls for a formal invitation, though it is not required. A formal invitation consists of three parts:

1 Main invitation. In the case of a Catholic confirmation, you'd include the occasion, where and when the Mass will be held, the church location, etc.

2 Smaller invitation to the party afterwards, including location.

3 Small response card with self-addressed envelope.

The phrasing should be formal: "Anthony and Carmela Soprano announce the Confirmation of their son, Anthony Soprano, Jr...." The invitations themselves can come in a variety of styles. Ask a stationery expert. He'll have all the answers.

SAMPLE CONFIRMATION PROGRAM

A confirmation program (ask your local stationery store to help out) is nice as a keepsake. Programs can be placed in the church vestibule in a basket or a tray, and likewise at home afterwards. The program guides the guest through the steps of the confirmation, but in addition, it's nice to add some personal touches. The following was included in AJ's confirmation program.

MY LIFE SO FAR
by
Anthony Soprano, Jr.

A lot of you probably know me as the obnoxious kid over at the Sopranos,' but there's more to me than that. I am a person who loves life with a capital L. I love food, I love free downloads, and I think all music and movies should be free to the people. I love all funny movies, and I love drumming like Keith Moon of The Who, who died tragically young. I have a talent for contact sports and may become a professional athlete someday. If not, I'm interested in the fields of video games, owning an arena football team like Bon Jovi, or something in the area of PR. I'm good with people – I can talk them into anything.

Thanks for coming to my confirmation party and thanks for your generous gift, whatever it is.

I'M HIS GODFATHER
by
Salvatore Bonpensiero

AJ asked me to introduce myself and so I will. I knew the kid's grandfather, Johnny Boy Soprano, from way back and have worked alongside his dad, Tony, for many, many lucrative years. I am so honored that they picked me for this job. I remember the day of birth like it was yesterday. The proud papa Tony couldn't stop grinning. He gave everyone a whole box of Cuban cigars. What a guy! If AJ grows up to be half the man his old man is, he'll be twice the man as me. Go get 'em kid. I'm behind you all the way.

A NOTE FROM "FATHER PHIL"

On behalf of Pope John Paul II and the 1.1 billion Catholics worldwide, I am most pleased to welcome Anthony, Jr. ("AJ") into our flock at Saint Peter and Paul's. His mother, Carmela, is a devout and hard-working parishioner especially active in our ladies' noontime speakers' series and whenever the calendar tells us it's "rummage sale time." His father is a generous contributor to our annual budget drive. If you would like to make a donation to the church in Anthony's name, please do, with our great appreciation and prayers. We will apply it to our exciting new after-school kids-at-risk program and you'll be profusely thanked in our weekly information handout, "Church News for *You!*" What better tribute to this fine young man than to see his church–*our* church–prosper and grow?

MUSIC ♪

Music is so personal, isn't it? But no party, gay or somber, is complete without it. Here and scattered throughout this book, I make a few modest musical suggestions to get you thinking. If you are unfamiliar with any of these, sample them. You might be pleasantly surprised.

For a baptism or confirmation, I would stay in the classical mode, featuring some of my favorite singers—Cecilia Bartoli, Maria Callas, and, in the more popular vein, Andrea Bocelli. Also, classical standards like Vivaldi's *Four Seasons* or Bach's *Brandenburg Concertos* work nicely.

sacred and profane, but the real meaning may have been lost in the shuffle. At a Catholic baptism, and probably in other traditions as well, a godparent or godparents, i.e., godmother and godfather, are non-relatives chosen to help guide the newborn through life and stay close to faith and family. They are back-up parents in a way, giving advice, teaching life skills, bearing witness to the child's growth and character. Nowadays, the right godparent can even help a young adult enter the world of education and business. They can write letters of recommendation for college admissions and set up much-sought-after internships in a chosen profession. A godparent, in other words, can open doors. In a

RULES OF GODFATHERING
by Silvio Dante

Being a godfather is hard work, don't kid yourself. The difference between a good godfather and a bad one is devotion. If your godson calls on a Saturday morning to say, "Let's go hiking," when you had already planned a day of golf, what are you going to do? Follow these simple rules and your question will be answered.

1 From baptism on, your presence is required at every religious turning point in this boy's life, all the way through seminary school, if that is his choosing. Start now to prepare a long toast for each occasion.

2 Get to know the kid. If he likes baseball cards, learn about baseball cards. If he likes to fight, teach him how to punch. That kind of thing.

3 Give him your private phone number, be it cellular or regular. If he calls you at 3 a.m., it's probably important. He may have gotten a girl in trouble or something and can't tell his old man. I've been there.

4 Religion aside, you are there for every "Big Day" in his life. His first T-ball game. His school Christmas sing-along. His first car. The day he gets out of rehab, should that be necessary. Sometimes you have to plan your whole life around this kid. Get used to it.

5 Live up to your financial commitment. From contributing to his college fund on a regular basis to buying him nice presents when required, godfathering can involve a large cash outlay. In his early twenties, the kid may need to borrow ten or twenty grand for an unspecified obligation. Loan it to him, without interest.

6 Finally, if something should happen to the boy's father, God forbid, you become his father, either for the duration or at least until a suitable stepfather enters the picture and takes over. If you know nothing about fathering, buy a book.

competitive world like ours, you need all the help you can get, and the well-connected godparent is, well, a godsend.

It's a distinct honor to be chosen as a godparent, a title usually reserved for a close family friend who will be steadfast in his or her love and loyalty. Unfortunately, AJ's godfather is no longer with us, robbing him of that special relationship that might have helped him through some rough times. A godparent must have been there from the beginning. You can't simply replace him or her if a fracture occurs in the relationship between parent and godparent.

Enough about tradition—let's have a party! For a confirmation celebration, I recommend a buffet with a few special touches. The buffet table is best situated in the center of a room, if possible, allowing access to the food from all sides. It's a good idea to create different levels of food presentation. Use a cake stand, for instance, to feature desserts. Take a wooden box, cover it with fabric, and put condiments on it. This is something most people don't think about and it's so easy. Try it. It adds a touch of class.

Traditional buffets often have a nice tablecloth, a floral centerpiece, sometimes candles, and, if you really want to impress your guests, an ice sculpture.

WINE SUGGESTIONS

I asked Artie Bucco to recommend someone who could provide expertise in the area of Southern Italian wines and he led me right to Charles Scicolone, wine director of Vino Italian Wines and Spirits in Manhattan. Following are some of Charles's suggestions to fit our confirmation menu. Look for them in your area. You won't be disappointed. *CS*

WINE SUGGESTIONS

Falanghina
{ a white wine from Campania }

Greco di Tufo
{ another white wine from Campania }

Aglianico
{ a red wine from Campania }

PARTY FAVORS

Favors for a baptism or confirmation usually allude to the religious significance of the event—rosaries, cross-shaped candles, pocket-sized Bibles, or other symbols of devotion. A nice presentation is to place the gifts in individual fabric-mesh drawstring bags or small tins and then arrange them on a table near the entrance. Add a small sign: "Please Take One."

TIPS ON HANDLING RAMBUNCTIOUS CHILDREN

by Janice Soprano Baccilieri

Being a mother of one and a stepmother of two, I know all too well how rowdy, ill-mannered children of guests can ruin a party and even damage precious heirlooms. Here's what I do. Feeling I have a special way with children, I first try to tune in to their wavelength and engage them creatively. For instance, if I find them trashing the house, I might locate some old cardboard boxes and say, "Make me a castle and invite me to high tea." Make-believe is so wonderfully childlike. A garage is also a good make-believe land. Just close the door and tell them they're in a big, dark cave.

If this doesn't work, I apply a mild form of fear, as in, "God will punish you if you don't behave at a confirmation party." Another technique: Bribe them. Give them disposable cameras to play with or promise them a big sack of candy for the ride home (but not before). Finally, if all else fails, I confront the parents, always speaking to them in a sympathetic tone, parent to parent. Unless they have "overcelebrated" and could care less about their offspring, they'll deal with the problem tout de suite. You could always hire a baby-sitter, but who wants the expense?

You could also snake a garland-style arrangement in and out of the dishes on the buffet and maybe, given the theme of the party, create a line of votive candles. If you use drip candles, watch the drips. You don't want to ruin a perfectly good spaghetti pie with an unintended crust of candle wax.

To create maximum visual effect for a special event like this, choose a single color scheme and stick to it. White is the simplest: white tablecloths, white candles, white napkins, even a white floral scheme. Flowers are important. You can create a strong impression by amassing different flowers of the same color family. Imagine a room full of pink roses, pink tulips, and pink peonies. If they are all in similar containers, it's all the more striking. In fact, try three of the same-shaped vases, but in varying heights. The idea is to have fun with it. Put flowers everywhere—the powder room, buffet table, side tables, and mantels. On a cost/impact basis, flowers are one of entertaining's greatest values.

How to arrange the food for a buffet? After all, you can't just throw it on the table and have people going back and forth deciding what to eat. There's actually a right way to do this, or at least an accepted way that professional caterers know to use (thank you, Charmaine Bucco, my professional-caterer friend). Plates should always be at the beginning, naturally, followed in order by salads and dressings, then side dishes, first entrée, second entrée, bread, condiments, and finally flatware rolled in napkins. If you have a dish where you only want guests to take a small portion, for whatever reason, place it at the end of this procession. Their plates will be already filled, allowing not much room for the special item.

A few other useful buffet tips: Cut the food into manageable portions before you set it out. You don't want people struggling with slicing up a whole chicken or tearing off a set of ribs while the line behind them waits. Slice chicken breasts into chunks; score casserole dishes like lasagne; snap ears of corn in half. Also, maximize eye appeal with garnishes like parsley or edible flowers from the grocery store (but never from the florist—they use pesticides), or artfully add in some curled strips of carrot or lemon rind. As with most things, food preparation is in the details. Don't get too fussy, but a few well-placed garnishes can make the difference between just food and an inviting buffet.

Most of us don't have the furnishings to accommodate a big affair like a confirmation party. So we rent. Before you talk to a vendor, decide what you really need. Is yours going to be a sit-down event or will a few long serving tables do the trick? Even if you want guests to sit and eat, many won't, so don't over-rent. On the other hand, many rental outfits now provide the whole package—china, flatware, wineglasses, tables, and chairs. This may bust your budget, but it can save you a lot of needless bother. Pick and choose what you need. It may just be sixty wineglasses.

Hopefully, your pre-planning is thorough enough to allow you to enjoy this transition point in the life of your child. A confirmation or coming-of-age party is an emotional moment for the parents, probably more so than for the child-cum-adult. Let a godparent or close family friend make the first toast. You'll be too busy wiping away the tears.

NEAPOLITAN CROSTINI

Serves 6

INGREDIENTS

2 ripe medium tomatoes, preferably New Jersey beefsteaks

½ teaspoon dried oregano

Salt and freshly ground pepper

12 thin slices Italian bread, preferably semolina bread

8 ounces fresh mozzarella, cut into 12 slices

12 anchovy fillets

Extra virgin olive oil

PREPARATION

Cut the tomatoes in half through the core and squeeze gently to extract the seeds and juice. Trim away the core. Chop the tomatoes into ½-inch pieces and toss them in a bowl with the oregano, and salt and pepper to taste.

Preheat the oven to 450°. Oil a large baking pan.

Arrange the bread slices on the pan. Toast the bread 5 minutes. Remove the pan from the oven, but leave it turned on.

Place a slice of mozzarella on top of each piece of bread, and then an anchovy. Spoon a little of the tomatoes on each. Drizzle with a few drops extra virgin olive oil.

Return the pan to the oven and bake 5 to 7 minutes, or until the cheese is slightly melted. Serve immediately.

SPAGHETTI PIE

Serves 8

INGREDIENTS

8 large eggs

½ cup freshly grated Pecorino Romano or Parmigiano-Reggiano

Freshly ground pepper

1 pound spaghetti or bucatini, cooked and drained

2 ounces sliced Genoa salami or soppressata, chopped

2 ounces sliced prosciutto or boiled ham, chopped

2 tablespoons olive oil

4 ounces provolone, chopped

PREPARATION

In a large bowl, beat the eggs, grated cheese, and pepper to taste. You will not need salt, because the meats and cheeses are salty. Add the spaghetti, salami, and prosciutto to the bowl and toss well.

Heat the oil in a 10-inch nonstick skillet over medium heat. Pour half of the pasta into the skillet. Scatter the provolone on top. Pour on the remaining spaghetti mixture.

Turn the heat to medium-low. Cover the pan and cook 5 minutes. Slide a spatula under the pie and lift it gently around the edges to allow some of the uncooked eggs to slide underneath. Cover and cook 10 minutes, or until the eggs are almost set and the bottom is golden.

Meanwhile, preheat the broiler.

Place the skillet under the broiler to brown the top and finish cooking the eggs, about 3 to 5 minutes more.

Run a spatula under the pie to loosen it. Lift the handle of the pan and slip the pie out onto a serving platter. Cut into wedges. Serve hot or at room temperature.

EGGPLANT ROLLATINI

Serves 8

INGREDIENTS

2 large eggplants (about 1¼ pounds each)

Salt

Olive oil

8 ounces fresh mozzarella, cut into ½-inch sticks

2 cups Tomato Sauce (page 32)

¼ cup freshly grated Pecorino Romano

PREPARATION

Cut the eggplant into ¼-inch-thick diagonal slices, so that they are as wide as possible. Layer the slices in a colander set over a plate, sprinkling each layer with salt. Cover the eggplant with another plate and a weight and let stand at least 30 minutes to drain the excess liquid.

Preheat the oven to 450°F.

Rinse the eggplant with cool water and pat dry with paper towels. Brush the eggplant slices on both sides with olive oil. Place them in a single layer on large baking sheets. Bake 10 minutes, or until very lightly browned on the bottom. Turn the slices and bake 5 to 10 minutes more, or until tender and very lightly browned. Remove the eggplant from the oven. Lower the oven temperature to 350°F.

Spoon a thin layer of sauce into a 13 x 9 x 2-inch baking dish. Place 1 piece of mozzarella across the end of each slice of eggplant. Roll up the eggplant and place the pieces seam side down in the dish.

Spoon the remaining sauce over the eggplant. Sprinkle with the grated cheese. Bake 25 minutes, or until the mozzarella is melted and the sauce is bubbling.

Serve hot.

CRUNCHY BAKED CHICKEN

Serves 4

INGREDIENTS

2 large eggs

1 tablespoon water

1 large garlic clove, minced

½ teaspoon dried oregano

1 teaspoon salt

¼ teaspoon freshly ground pepper

2 cups plain dry bread crumbs, preferably homemade from Italian bread

½ cup freshly grated Pecorino Romano

¼ cup olive oil

1 chicken (about 3½ pounds), cut into 8 pieces, skin removed (or you can use skinless chicken parts)

PREPARATION

In a shallow dish, beat together the eggs, water, garlic, oregano, salt, and pepper.

On a piece of wax paper, mix the crumbs with the cheese. Drizzle with the oil and stir until blended.

Preheat the oven to 400°F.

Dip the chicken in the egg mixture, then roll the pieces in the crumb mixture, patting it so that it will stick. Place the chicken on a rack, skin side up, and let the coating dry for 15 minutes.

Oil a baking sheet and arrange the chicken pieces on it. Bake 20 minutes. With tongs, carefully turn the chicken pieces, so as not to disturb the coating. Bake 20 minutes more, or until the chicken is browned and cooked through when cut into at the thickest part.

Serve hot or at room temperature.

GREEN BEAN, POTATO, AND RED ONION SALAD

Serves 6

INGREDIENTS

1½ pounds green beans, trimmed

Salt

4 to 6 medium Yukon Gold or red-skin potatoes

2 tablespoons chopped fresh basil or flat-leaf parsley

½ cup olive oil

3 to 4 tablespoons red wine vinegar

Freshly ground pepper

2 tablespoons capers, rinsed and drained

1 medium red onion, thinly sliced

PREPARATION

Bring a large saucepan of water to a boil. Add the green beans and salt to taste. Cook until the beans are tender, about 8 minutes. Drain the beans in a colander and cool them under cold running water. Drain and pat dry. Cut into bite-sized pieces.

Put the potatoes in a medium saucepan with cold water to cover and salt to taste.

Cover and bring to a simmer over medium heat. Cook until the potatoes are tender when pierced with a sharp knife, about 20 minutes. Drain and let cool slightly. Peel the potatoes and cut into cubes.

In a large bowl, whisk together the oil, vinegar, and salt and pepper to taste. Stir in the capers. Add the green beans, potatoes, and onion and toss well.

Serve at room temperature.

CHOCOLATE FUDGE SHEET CAKE

Serves 12

INGREDIENTS

2 cups sugar

2 cups all-purpose flour

1 teaspoon baking soda

¼ teaspoon salt

8 tablespoons (1 stick) unsalted butter, cut into pieces

1 cup water

⅓ cup unsweetened cocoa powder

1 teaspoon instant espresso powder

2 large eggs

½ cup sour cream, buttermilk, or plain yogurt

2 teaspoons pure vanilla extract

MOCHA FUDGE FROSTING

½ cup heavy cream

4 tablespoons (½ stick) unsalted butter

2 tablespoons light corn syrup

1 teaspoon instant espresso powder

8 ounces bittersweet chocolate, chopped or broken into small pieces

PREPARATION

Place a rack in the center of the oven. Preheat the oven to 350°F. Grease and flour a 13 x 9 x 2-inch baking pan. Invert the pan and tap out the excess flour.

Sift together the sugar, flour, baking soda, and salt into a large mixing bowl.

Melt the butter with the water, cocoa powder, and espresso powder in a medium saucepan over medium heat, stirring until the mixture comes to a boil. Pour the liquid over the dry ingredients and stir until smooth.

In a small bowl, whisk the eggs, sour cream, and vanilla until smooth. Scrape the mixture into the large bowl and stir just until blended.

Pour the batter into the prepared pan and smooth the surface with a rubber spatula. Bake until a toothpick inserted in the center comes out clean, about 35 minutes. Let the cake cool in the pan on a rack about 5 minutes. Invert the cake onto the rack to cool completely.

To make the frosting, in a medium saucepan, heat the cream, butter, corn syrup, and espresso until simmering. Remove the pan from the heat, add the chocolate, and let stand a few minutes to soften. Stir until completely smooth. Chill, stirring occasionally, until the frosting is just thick enough to spread.

Place the cake upside down on a tray or board. Scrape the frosting onto the cake and spread it evenly over the top and sides with a rubber spatula.

Let the cake set at cool room temperature at least 1 hour before cutting. Or refrigerate until the frosting is set, then wrap loosely in foil and store overnight. (To keep the foil from touching the frosting, poke a few toothpicks into the top of the cake before wrapping. Be sure to remove the picks before serving the cake.)

23

Chapter 2

GRADUATION PARTIES

There are few events as momentous in a young person's life as high school or college graduation. Especially if you come from a family like ours, where college was not traditionally an option, the glory of graduation is certainly an event to celebrate with loved ones. Of course, by the ages of eighteen to twenty-two, kids have their own ideas of what does or does not make for a great party. You may need to remind them, gently, that this is not a party for *their* friends—they can have those anytime—but a party for friends *and* all the people who nurtured them into adulthood, most of all, their parents. My advice is to allow the graduate to play a part in the preparation but not take over all the details. Find a happy middle ground between an all-night rave and dinner with Grandpa. It's in there somewhere, trust me.

Beginning with the invitation, make it easy on yourself. Kids today communicate almost exclusively via e-mail and instant messaging (IM), so don't use the mail, use the Internet. E-mailing actually allows you to avoid all the work involved in designing, printing, labeling, and stamping a "snail mail" invitation, leaving you more time to plan the actual party! E-mail invitations are fast, fun, and efficient. Go to an e-mail invitation web site (or

with something that reflects her tastes. Your male grad, if given a vote, might choose black as the dominant color. Try to dissuade him of this morbid choice.

The mood of the party is most likely casual, so decorate accordingly. Give the teenagers and young adults a place to hang out that befits their interests, which usually run to video games, borderline-tasteful TV, or maybe cheesy horror movies on DVDs. Have stuff for them to sit on like floor cushions or beanbag chairs. Have enough snack items to feed a small army, then double the amount. You could even string up novelty lights as an offbeat touch.

This is not the generation likely to have your child do it) and just follow the instructions. To find such a site, go to your favorite search engine, like Google or Yahoo!, and type in "e-mail invitations"; Evite.com is one I've used. The guest usually receives an e-mail attachment that looks like an envelope. They then click that open, and there's an electronic invite, identical to a paper one, with whatever graphics and information you choose. In addition, the invitees can RSVP electronically so you don't have to be calling the entire list to double-check. You can, on the other hand, just hit a button and remind them all the day before.

Remember the notion, discussed in Chapter One, of building a decorative scheme around a dominant color? Let the grad choose that color or colors. This might be reflected in flowers, crepe paper, paper lanterns, paper tablecloths and napkins, and other items of décor. A graduating male probably won't care unless you pick something embarrassing like baby pink or baby blue, but your daughter or niece might want to weigh in

want to play card games or charades, though you could always suggest it. More likely, your grad will want to pick a favorite all-time movie for all to watch, perhaps one he or she and their friends just loved when they were ten or eleven. Think of '80s movie events like *The Breakfast Club, The Karate Kid,* or *Uncle Buck.* Hit upon the right

DVD, and that could be a big feature of the party right there. You might even pick up a few décor ideas from the movie.

This might embarrass your grad, but it could be fun for everyone else: turn school mementos into items of décor. Blow up a high school football or softball picture and display it like a blowup of a professional star. Display school jerseys, pennants, election posters, and the three hundred soccer trophies you've dutifully saved as if the whole house, or at least part of it, was a Hall of Fame exhibit. You could also create an achievement board, using poster board and an easel, to showcase everything from an award-winning sixth-grade essay to his or her monthly cell-phone bill. Don't try to be too "hip" or blatantly hype your kid—all kids hate that—but find things in his or her life that will make everyone smile, even the writer of that sixth-grade essay.

If your grad is anything like my grad, the right music is serious business. They do not want to hear their hammy uncle sing "Moon River," in English or Italian, and will probably balk at your favorite background choices of Andrea Bocelli or *Essential Baroque Masterpieces*. The easiest solution is to let them program their own music, as long as the lyrics don't include cop-killing or obscene references to female body parts. There are two easy ways to do this. One, just plug the grad's portable MP3 player into your stereo system. If you don't know MP3 from NBC, ask them. Secondly, you could have the grad just burn a CD selection of their favorite songs and play it back on a conventional CD player. If you don't know what "burn" means, again, don't worry—they'll know. Personally I didn't know any of this until my son, AJ, after some considerable arm-twisting, spent an evening educating his clueless mom.

Of course, the big issue with anything involving teenagers is alcohol. If your party is for a college graduate, your choice is soft drinks versus, say, beer or wine. You know your twenty-one-year-old better

RULES ON THE GIVING OF MONEY
by Christopher Moltisanti

Everybody likes money. It's the one thing you never have to return to the store. In my particular milieu, the giving of money is a time-honored practice and it demands a certain amount of what you might call finesse. If you do it wrong, you will look like a complete idiot, trust me.

- Always give cash. No checks, IOUs, travel vouchers, gift certificates (very popular these days), or free car-wash coupons. Cash.

- Choose the right amount. If you give a high school grad $1,000, you're a sucker. If you plan to give him two fives, don't show up at the party.

- Put it in a plain legal-sized white envelope. Do not put your name on it in florid script, nor include a stupid "To a Cool Grad!" greeting card.

- Do not make a big show of the giving. Think of it like passing a secret note to a spy or making a drug buy on the street, like you've no doubt seen on many a TV crime show. Locate a dark corner for the handoff, followed by the requisite bear hug.

- Finally, don't think that just because your girlfriend bought the kid a glow-in-the-dark digital watch that you're off the hook. At least in my crowd, you don't give the envelope, people will know. And you, chump, will be scorned and shamed.

GIFTS AND PARTY FAVORS
by Meadow Soprano

Having been through this ritual a few times, I think I know what *not* to give someone graduating high school or college. No alarm clocks, please. No dictionaries or thesauruses; it's all online for free, plus that's why God made Spell Check. No stationery, pen and pencil sets, or even watches, unless, of course, it's Cartier or Rolex (just kidding). What to give? New consumer technology is a safe bet: a digital camera, wireless headphones, maybe a PDA (personal digital assistant) or an MP3 player. These devices change rapidly, so do a little research before you buy; you may be a week behind. Portable furniture is great too—I got a bean-bag chair at my high school graduation party that I still have and love. And, of course, no self-respecting grad ever turned their nose up at money.

As for party favors, here are a few I've gotten and liked. A friend took a canvas laundry bag, always useful, and filled it with all kinds of stuff. Your own bag could include: a goofy T-shirt to commemorate the occasion (maybe a picture of the high school principal or something risqué like "Everyone Loves a Catholic Girl"); gift certificates for free ring tones, MP3 downloads, even an online emporium like Amazon; an iPod case or a portable CD holder; a Magic Eight Ball; a subscription to the hometown newspaper; and an eyeshade for sleeping late.

than I do. It's your job to keep alcohol consumption in check, especially for those driving home. To help do this, think of something that might engage them more than Jell-O shots. Rent a karaoke machine for the day and drag Aunt Sarah on stage to sing "Smells Like Teen Spirit." Rent a four-for-a-dollar photo booth. Book a psychic or a tarot card reader to tell your graduate and friends what the future holds for them. Prices vary by area, but mind readers usually run about $100 an hour. All of these services can be found online, in the Yellow Pages, or through word-of-mouth referrals.

Finally, work up a good toast for your young achiever. You could go all out and narrate a fifteen-minute slide show of every bubble bath and sleep-over photo you ever took, but just a heartfelt tribute to their wonderful spirit and good sense will do, even if their good sense is still evolving. Remember, you're not there to embarrass them, but to honor them. And to honor yourself as well.

THE FEAR OF HOSTESSING

I asked a family friend, therapist Dr. Jennifer Melfi, if she had any thoughts on why some people are too mortified to entertain at home. To my delight, she had just returned from a weeklong conference on Acute Social Anxiety Disorders, including a panel on this very topic. Here are her reflections.

DR. JENNIFER MELFI, M.D., M.A., M.F.T.

Dear Carmela:

I finally found a minute to collect my thoughts re the subject we discussed. I call it "party anxiety" and plan to develop a peer-group paper on this debilitating fear. But for now, here are some cursory observations.

"The need to please." It is so ingrained in the mind of the modern party giver—usually female but not always—that the very idea of opening her doors to friends and family is a source of deep psychic pain. Many people simply avoid this pain by never hosting anything bigger than chicken-in-a-box for four. Those who contemplate a more elaborate soiree feel deeply inadequate. Their shabby house isn't up to snuff. Their microwave-centered food skills aren't up to snuff. The only decorating they've ever done was a cowboy-themed birthday party for a four-year-old. They feel instantly self-conscious, dull, boring, and ugly. Yes, ugly. Many say, "I'm too unattractive to host a big party. The hostess is always the prettiest one in the room."

On the surface, this seems silly, doesn't it? I mean, parties are work, for sure, but they aren't brain surgery. Well, fear of flying or fear of unsanitary public toilets seems silly, too, until you yourself are gripped by this fear. Don't laugh at your friend with "party anxiety." Give her a new perspective. Give her the cognitive tools to overcome her fears and enjoy the moment.

Personally, I see party anxiety as performance anxiety. The phobic in question sees opening her house and lifestyle to others as tantamount to a one-person stage show entitled "Now You Know the Real Me." So, let's just run with the stage metaphor. How do you prepare for a performance? You rehearse. In a lighthearted spirit, walk your nervous friend through all the steps of a modest house party as if she were a little girl playing with her dollhouse. There's no fear in that—it's harmless make-believe. Once she gets into the "game" of party planning, she'll begin to realize that it's not the overwhelming or onerous task she imagined. It's a step-by-step process. What do you like to eat? There's the menu. What's your favorite flower? There's the décor. What's the most fun dress you've ever owned? There's your outfit. Who do you really like and not just tolerate? There's your guest list.

If all goes well, the subject begins to see the party unfold in her imagination in the same way an Olympic runner visualizes crossing the finish line first or a second-rate actor visualizes his acceptance speech for the Academy Awards. When she sees it, she starts to believe in it, and when she starts to believe in the party, she starts to believe in herself.

Of course, planning a party and the actual job of hosting one are two different things. But, if you can help your friend get through the steps above, you're at least halfway there.

I hope this helps, and good luck with your book project,

Dr. Jennifer Melfi

LITTLE CHICKEN MEATBALLS

Serves 8

INGREDIENTS

½ cup fresh bread crumbs made from Italian or French bread (with the crusts removed)

¼ cup milk

1 pound ground chicken or turkey

1 large egg, beaten

½ cup freshly grated Parmigiano-Reggiano

2 tablespoons coarsely chopped pine nuts

2 tablespoons finely chopped fresh flat-leaf parsley, plus more for garnish

1 teaspoon salt

Freshly ground pepper

1½ cups Tomato Sauce (page 32)

PREPARATION

Preheat the oven to 350°F. Lightly oil a large roasting pan.

Soak the bread crumbs in the milk in a small bowl until it is absorbed. Lightly squeeze the bread crumbs.

In a large bowl, combine the soaked bread, chicken, egg, cheese, pine nuts, parsley, salt, and pepper to taste. Mix well with your hands.

Rinse your hands with cold water. Shape the mixture into 1-inch balls. (It is important to make them all the same size so that they cook evenly.) Place the balls in the prepared pan.

Bake the meatballs until lightly browned and cooked through, about 10 to 12 minutes. (You can make these a day ahead of time. Let cool, then cover and refrigerate until ready to serve.)

In a large skillet, bring the tomato sauce to a simmer. Add the meatballs and simmer 10 minutes, stirring occasionally. Add a little water if the sauce is very thick.

Serve hot, with a sprinkle of parsley.

31

TOMATO SAUCE

Makes about 3 cups

INGREDIENTS

1 small onion, chopped

1 garlic clove, chopped

2 tablespoons olive oil

One 28-ounce can Italian-style crushed tomatoes

2 fresh basil leaves, torn into bits

Salt and freshly ground pepper

PREPARATION

In a medium saucepan, cook the onion and garlic in the oil over medium heat until tender and golden, about 10 minutes.

Add the tomatoes, basil, and salt and pepper to taste. Bring to a simmer and cook 10 to 15 minutes, or until the sauce is thickened.

Serve hot with meatballs, pasta, eggplant, etc.

(This sauce can be made up to 3 days ahead of time; cover and store in the refrigerator. The sauce can also be frozen.)

EGGPLANT FRITTERS

Makes about 30

INGREDIENTS

2 medium eggplants (about 1 pound each)

Salt

2 large eggs, beaten

¾ cup plus 1½ cups plain dry bread crumbs, preferably homemade from Italian bread

½ cup freshly grated Pecorino Romano

¼ cup chopped fresh flat-leaf parsley

Freshly ground pepper

Vegetable oil for frying

PREPARATION

Trim off the stems of the eggplants and cut them lengthwise in half. Bring a large pot of water to a boil. Add the eggplant and salt to taste. Cook until tender, about 15 minutes. Place the eggplant in a colander to drain and cool completely.

When they are cool, squeeze the eggplants gently to extract excess liquid. Chop them very fine and place them in a large bowl. Add the eggs, ¾ cup of the bread crumbs, the cheese, parsley, 1 teaspoon salt, and pepper to taste. Spread the remaining 1½ cups bread crumbs on a piece of wax paper.

Shape the mixture into 1½-inch patties about ½ inch thick. Roll the patties in the bread crumbs, patting the crumbs on well. Place the patties on a baking sheet to set up, about 15 minutes.

Pour oil to about a ½-inch depth into a large heavy skillet. Heat over medium heat until a bit of the crumbs sizzle when dropped in the oil. Carefully place some of the patties in the pan, leaving a little space between them. Fry them, turning once, until evenly browned, about 10 minutes. Transfer the fritters to paper towels to drain, then serve immediately or keep warm in a low oven while frying the remainder. (These are good plain for an appetizer, but you can also serve them with Tomato Sauce, page 32, for a main dish.)

STROMBOLI BREAD

Makes three 12-inch loaves

INGREDIENTS

1 package (2½ teaspoons) active dry yeast

1½ cups warm water (100° to 110°F)

About 4 cups all-purpose flour

2 teaspoons salt

8 ounces sliced mild provolone

8 ounces sliced capicola, salami, or boiled ham

1 egg yolk, beaten with 2 tablespoons water

PREPARATION

In a small bowl, sprinkle the yeast over the water. Let stand until the yeast is creamy, about 5 minutes. Stir until the yeast dissolves.

In a heavy-duty mixer or food processor, combine 3½ cups of the flour and the salt. Add the yeast and process or mix until a soft dough forms. Remove the dough from the bowl and knead until smooth and elastic, about 2 minutes, adding more flour as necessary to make a moist but not sticky dough.

Oil a large bowl. Put the dough in the bowl, turning it once to oil the top. Cover with plastic wrap. Place in a warm, draft-free spot and let rise until doubled, about 1½ hours.

Remove the dough from the bowl and flatten it with your hands to eliminate air bubbles. Cut the dough into 3 even pieces and shape each piece into a ball. Place the balls on a floured surface, several inches apart, and cover with plastic wrap. Let rise 1 hour, or until doubled.

Preheat the oven to 400°F. Oil a large baking sheet.

On a lightly floured surface, roll out one ball of dough with a rolling pin into a 14-inch circle. Arrange one-third of the cheese slices over the dough, leaving a 1-inch border all around. Top with one-third of the meat. Tightly roll up the dough and filling like a sausage. Pinch the seam to seal. Place the roll seam side down on the baking sheet. Tuck the ends of the dough under the roll. Make 2 more rolls with the remaining ingredients.

Brush the rolls with the egg yolk mixture. With a knife, cut 4 shallow slashes evenly spaced in the top of each roll. Bake 30 to 35 minutes, or until golden brown.

Transfer to wire racks to cool slightly.

Serve the bread warm, cut into diagonal slices. Or cool completely before wrapping in foil and storing. The loaves can be kept in the refrigerator overnight or stored in the freezer up to 1 month.

RED, WHITE, AND GREEN SALAD

Serves 8 to 10

INGREDIENTS

1 head green leaf lettuce, trimmed, washed, and dried
1 large head radicchio, trimmed, washed, and dried
3 Belgian endives, trimmed, washed, and dried
⅓ cup extra virgin olive oil
2 to 3 tablespoons balsamic vinegar
Salt and freshly ground pepper

PREPARATION

Tear the lettuce and radicchio into bite-sized pieces and put in a salad bowl. You should have about 8 cups.

Cut the endives crosswise into 1-inch pieces. Add them to the bowl.

In a small jar with a tight-fitting lid, shake together the oil, vinegar, and salt and pepper to taste.

Just before serving, shake the dressing again, and drizzle it over the salad. Toss well. Taste for seasoning. Serve immediately.

ANTIPASTO PLATTER

Serves 8 to 12

INGREDIENTS

1 small head green leaf lettuce, trimmed, washed, and dried

4 ounces sliced hot or sweet capicola

4 ounces sliced soppressata or other Italian-style salami

4 ounces thinly sliced imported prosciutto, such as prosciutto di Parma

4 ounces sliced mortadella

8 ounces imported sharp provolone, cut into wedges

8 ounces ricotta salata, cut into wedges

FOR GARNISH

Imported black olives, such as Gaela or oil-cured

Cracked green Sicilian olives

Pickled peperoncini or other hot peppers

Giardiniera (mixed pickled vegetables)

Roasted peppers

Anchovy fillets

Marinated sun-dried tomatoes, artichoke hearts, or mushrooms

PREPARATION

Make a bed of the lettuce leaves on a large serving platter. Loosely fold or roll up the sliced meats, and arrange the meats and cheeses neatly in rows or in groups on the lettuce. Garnish the platter with your choice of olives, pickled peppers, giardiniera, roasted peppers, anchovies, and marinated sun-dried tomatoes, artichoke hearts, or mushrooms. Cover and refrigerate until ready to serve.

Serve with Italian bread or breadsticks.

ALMOND ROLL WITH STRAWBERRY SAUCE

Serves 10 to 12

INGREDIENTS

⅔ cup all-purpose flour

½ teaspoon baking powder

4 large eggs, separated

¾ cup sugar

1 teaspoon pure vanilla extract

¼ teaspoon almond extract

Pinch of salt

½ cup very finely chopped toasted almonds

Confectioners' sugar

FILLING

1½ cups heavy cream

2 tablespoons sugar

1 teaspoon pure vanilla extract

STRAWBERRY SAUCE

2 pints fresh strawberries, rinsed and hulled

6 tablespoons sugar, or more to taste

1 tablespoon fresh lemon juice, or
  more to taste

Strawberries for garnish

PREPARATION

Place a rack in the center of the oven. Preheat the oven to 375°F. Butter a 17 x 12 x 1-inch jelly-roll pan or baking sheet.

Sift the flour and baking powder onto a piece of wax paper.

In a large mixer bowl, beat the egg yolks until light. Gradually beat in ½ cup of the sugar. Add the extracts. Holding the wax paper like a funnel, add the flour mixture, using a rubber spatula to gently fold it in.

In a large bowl with clean beaters, beat the egg whites and salt until foamy. Gradually add the remaining ¼ cup sugar and beat until soft peaks form when the beaters are lifted. Gently fold the whites and nuts into the egg yolk mixture.

Spread the batter in the prepared pan. Bake 12 to 14 minutes, or until lightly browned on top and the cake springs back when touched in the center.

Meanwhile, spread a large lint-free kitchen towel (not terry cloth) out on a kitchen counter. Dust it with confectioners' sugar. As soon as the cake is ready, run a knife around the edges and invert it onto the towel. Roll up the cake, in the towel, from one of the long sides. Place the rolled-up cake on a rack to cool.

Place a large mixing bowl and beaters in the refrigerator. (This will help the cream to whip better.) When you are ready to fill the cake, put the cream, sugar, and vanilla in

the bowl. Whip on high speed until soft peaks form when the beaters are lifted.

Unroll the cake, leaving it on the towel. Beginning at one of the long sides, spread it with the cream, stopping about 2 inches short of the other long side. (Leaving a space at the end will allow room for the cream to spread when the cake is rolled up.)

Reroll the cake, stopping while the cake is still on the towel. If the ends of the roll are uneven, trim them on the diagonal with a serrated knife, using a sawing motion. Using the towel to lift it, place the cake seam side down on a serving plate or tray. Remove the towel. Sprinkle the cake with confectioners' sugar. Cover and refrigerate at least 1 hour, or overnight, before serving.

To make the sauce, in a food processor or blender, combine all of the ingredients. Process or blend until smooth. Taste and add more sugar and/or lemon juice if needed. You should have about 2 cups. Use immediately, or cover and chill up to 24 hours.

To serve the cake, cut it into 1-inch slices. Serve with the sauce and fresh strawberries for garnish.

Chapter 3

FIT FOR A BRIDE
SHOWERS AND RECEPTIONS

There is no way, in one chapter of one entertaining book, that I can even scratch the surface of all the information out there about staging weddings, wedding receptions, wedding showers, wedding rehearsal dinners, wedding midnight snacks, or all the other events, large and small, that surround the modern nuptials. There are wedding magazines, wedding Internet sites, and a full-blown wedding-a-week on the morning TV talk shows. Let's face it, America is wedding-crazy. We love the bond of marriage.

And for good reason. Along with childbirth, it is the most hope-filled event in a person's life. Although modern weddings are often satirized and belittled on TV and in the movies, in the end of even the silliest comedies, there is a moment where we all go, "Awww!" And when the credits roll, we all feel like proud in-laws.

Weddings, like Christmas and Super Bowl Sunday, are now big business in America, which, for the individual bride and/or bride's parents, may add pressure and reduce pleasure. So my humble purpose here is to reduce pressure and add pleasure, with an Italian-American flavoring, of course. You don't have to hire an overbearing wedding consultant, and you don't have to spend a fortune to draw friends and family together in a joyous celebra-

that Tony's mother, Livia, forgot my name when she made a toast to our union. She called me Carmina. Like everyone else, she was probably flustered by all the excitement.

On my parents' big day in the 1940s, the first thing to remember is that no one in the Italian-American community at that time had any money. The typical nuptial event was called a "football wedding." A couple would be married in a local church, then the group would retreat to a local banquet hall, maybe the American Legion or Knights of Columbus, or even an empty apartment in the building, to eat, dance, drink, and make fools of themselves. There were no tables and no plates, just chairs brought from home, or even borrowed from the local funeral parlor, to sit on (the undertaker didn't charge, because he wanted the family's business). There was little or no décor, maybe a few streamers, and certainly no coordinated color scheme.

The food? Football-shaped cold sandwiches filled with *gabagool* (capicola), salami, ham, and cheese, and maybe tuna salad, wrapped in wax paper. The sandwiches were pre-made by friends of the bride's family, then hauled in big boxes to the reception, where they would be tossed, one at a time, to the hungry guests. They were called football weddings for two reasons, or so I've been

tion of matrimony. That doesn't mean you serve crackers and cheese. There's a middle ground—style and elegance at a reasonable price. Operating in this middle arena also allows you to turn what has become a commercial endeavor back into a personal one.

When I think back on my parents' and grandparents' lives, I begin to realize how out of control the present-day wedding ritual has become. My own wedding was a raucous but modest affair—the ceremony took place at St. Peter and Paul's Church, the same church we attend today, and the reception was a potluck affair at Tony's parents' house in West Orange. The only thing that really sticks in my mind, besides the warm glow of holy matrimony, is

MUSIC ♪

Love songs, what else? I, of course, favor the Italian love song as sung by Frank Sinatra, Dean Martin, Tony Bennett, Jerry Vale, Al Martino, or even Perry Como (I'm dating myself!). Or try something by Burt Bacharach. That guy can't write a bad song.

Theme Showers

In the old days, shower gifts were essentials, from pots and pans to sewing kits. Today most young people already have those common household items. Why not throw a theme shower, where the gifts are offbeat, unexpected, and often original? Here are five examples.

Recipe Shower

Each guest brings a treasured family recipe and some of the ingredients or equipment needed to make it. If your grandmother makes the best cannoli east of Sorrento, bring her the recipe, a special bottle of Italian wine for flavoring, a good flour sifter, and a set of cannoli forms. The bride may never get around to making cannolis, but she'll use the sifter and enjoy the wine.

Honeymoon Lingerie Shower

This one is self-explanatory. The idea is give intimate items the bride would probably never buy for herself: sexy pajamas, thongs, teddies, camisoles, bed jackets, and robes, to name but a few. If you want to turn up the heat a little, hold the shower at a local lingerie shop and nudge the blushing bride into a little modeling. The pictures will be pure gold.

Day-of-Beauty Shower

Host the shower at a local day spa or similar kind of "pamper-torium" and let everyone indulge in the true luxury of spa care. Depending on your budget, you could limit the program to a Swedish massage and sauna time or extend it to manicures, facials, waxing, and other bodily pleasures. The bride-to-be gets the deluxe treatment, of course, along with gifts that will help her relax for a long time to come: bath towels, bath salts, massage oils, even a towel warmer or a small pillow for relaxing the neck. There are special oils for romantic relaxation, but you may have already thought of that for the lingerie shower.

Travel Shower

A shower organized around travel items. The list is endless, depending on where the couple of honor may be traveling for their honeymoon or wish to travel in the future. There are the practical gifts like luggage, travel clocks, and tuck-away umbrellas, but there are also those gifts that inspire people to travel: guidebooks, coffee table books on the hills of Naples or New England in the fall, certificates for language lessons, even a bound travel journal or a beautiful map.

Garden Shower

If the couple-to-be already owns a house, a garden-themed party, perhaps held in a picturesque residential or public garden, could be perfect. Presents might include: a beautiful handmade flower pot; a stunning picture-filled book on landscaping or gardening 101; a shiny new soil tiller or ornamental birdbath. You could give every guest a packet of exotic flower seeds to plant in their own backyard. I don't know about you, but when summer comes to our area, we live in our backyard and the garden only adds to the pleasure. That's why they call New Jersey "The Garden State"!

told by my uncle-in-law Corrado Soprano. One, the sandwiches looked like footballs; and two, you'd catch one like a football and if you didn't like the particular kind of sandwich you were given, you could "pass" it to someone who did.

There may have been a local live band who would play Italian dance music for free sandwiches. The bride was given a plate that she threw down on the floor. The plate

shattered, of course, and all the pieces were collected and counted. The number of pieces, or so went the superstition, equaled the number of years the marriage would last.

However, we live now, not in 1946, and cold cuts in wax paper today would be considered embarrassingly cheap and miserly. But there's still room for sanity. Let's focus on showers. Sometimes these pre-wedding events are more relaxed and

MY PERFECT WEDDING
by Janice Soprano Baccilieri

My sister-in-law Carmela asked me to imagine a perfect wedding, or maybe I suggested the idea myself. In any case, weddings, to me, are as much about fantasy and self-expression as they are about guest lists and dinette sets. It's an opportunity for the romantic and artistic bride to stage a theatrical production of one's own creation, populated by one's own loved ones, and dedicated to the theme of enduring love.

First I would hold the wedding in a forest, far away from the artificiality of pomp or circumstance. As guests entered a cathedral of pines, they would pass an ancient wishing well where they could deposit small presents or deep thoughts about life and love. The wedding party per se would consist of the bride and groom, dressed in simple peasant nuptial costumes, and a half a dozen small children, all dressed like pre-Raphaelite wood nymphs. Guests would sit on a floor of pine needles as the children strewed daisy petals and four-leaf clovers over their heads. The music would be a single flute or a soprano saxophonist, not unlike Kenny G, accompanied by the natural sounds of the forest primeval. Ideally, I would love for the whole ceremony to be done in the nude, but unfortunately, the time for that kind of pagan openness has long passed.

The bride and groom would, of course, write their own vows, preferably as verse, like dueling Shakespearian love sonnets. Knowing them well, I would compose and perform a single love song in their honor. Once performed, the song would never be sung again. It would reside only in the hearts of the newly wedded, for as long as their marriage endured.

Again, if this were a more freedom-loving age, the whole congregation would then gather around a nearby natural lake or hot spring, disrobe, and frolic innocently in the water. Barring that, we'd move to a beautiful flaxen field, drink wine from jugs and eat meat off the bone, and engage in a frenzied Dionysian communal dance that would continue far into the starry night. We would fall asleep where we collapsed and awaken to the promise of new love on a new day in a new world.

I now pronounce you Adam and Eve.

free-form than the full-blown, lockstep scenario of the wedding. The bride-to-be is "showered" with good wishes and gifts from her closest friends and family. Bridal showers can take place anywhere from six months to a couple of days before the wedding, but two months prior is standard. This gives the bride-to-be a little breathing space to send thank-you notes for the shower before she is hit with the countdown to the big event.

Guests invited to a shower should be invited to the wedding, but not everyone coming to the wedding needs to be invited to the shower. Sometimes this gets a little tricky, but there are no rules when it comes to whether or not you *need* to invite someone you *have* to invite. You're on your own in that department. Traditionally, family members didn't throw the main bridal shower. It was considered bad form, as if they were saying, "Bring our darling daughter wedding presents, but first cough up a decent shower present, too." In the past, the job of organizing the shower fell to the maid of honor or some other close friend. If this is impractical, e.g., the maid of honor lives in Hawaii and the shower is in Newark, then bend the rules as you see fit.

It's perfectly acceptable for the shower invitation to include information about where guests can purchase gifts and even what kinds of gifts are preferred (see "Theme Showers"). It's perfectly acceptable to send shower invitations to people you know can't attend, for whatever reason. It's a nice way of telling them that they were in your thoughts at this life juncture.

My décor for an ideal shower would be romantic flowers and nice china and crystal. Think of floral arrangements using Dutch roses in dusty and burnt-pink hues, or sweet peas, or deep-pink peonies. Find some small silver-plated cups to use as vases, and let each guest take one home as a party favor. Other party favor ideas would include bottled bath salts, which I love; tins of exotic teas; little boxes of high-end chocolates; or small bags full of scented soaps shaped like rosebuds. These are some of my favorite little luxuries. Discover your own. And, again, the Internet is your friend, with hundreds of web sites devoted to this purpose.

Everything at the post-wedding reception is a bit more lush, even over the top, but some of the general guidelines used for a shower still apply. The flowers should be romantic and effusive. Place them everywhere at a reception, along, perhaps,

HOW TO GIVE A TOAST
by Peter Paul "Paulie Walnuts" Gualtieri

I am not a professional toastmaster, but I am usually the first person after the pre-designated toasters to stand and speak my mind. Actually, I like to toast. I often prepare and rehearse the right words the night before. Then it comes out of my mouth spontaneously and sincerely. If you can't do that, at least do this:

1 Wait your turn. There's a specific order to these things that cannot be violated at a reception: best man first; then groom; then bride, if she wants; then father of the bride; then father of the groom; and so on. Unless you're one of those people, have another drink and be patient.

2 Quietly stand and ask for attention. No clinking of glasses, wolf whistles, or, "Hey, I'm talkin' here!" joke lines. Show a little class for once in your life.

3 Never say, "You know, I've never done this before," or, "Boy, am I nervous, I'm sweatin' like a pig." No one cares. Just get on with it.

4 Say something nice and personal. Avoid the standard crap like, "Here's to two wonderful people," or "I second what that guy just said." If you have nothing witty or heartwarming to add, don't stand up in the first place.

5 Here are a couple of ways people I know end a toast. "*Salut'!*" is always good. It means "to your health." Or, there's always "*Cent'anni!*" It means "a hundred years" — i.e., "May you live that long." If you want to strike a religious note, end with "*E che Dio ti benedica*," or "God bless you." Who can argue with that?

6 Finally, make it short, my friend. It's a toast, for chrissakes, not an address to Congress.

with rented palms to brighten up bare corners. The favors can be more extravagant: individual potted orchids, say, with name tags/place cards; Jordan almonds in favor boxes tied with personalized ribbon or in vellum bags bearing the names of the bride and groom; or scented candles in small glass jars etched with the date of the wedding.

Think up a dramatic centerpiece, like a kissing-swan ice sculpture or giant vases of calla lilies. Or go a step further and erect a 1950s wedding staple: a champagne fountain made of tiered champagne glasses. Create an outlandish focal point that the whole party can dance around.

The style of menu I prefer for a shower is light on the entrée and a little indulgent on the desserts. Along with the main items, think of small touches like appetizers or individual cups of crudités like baby carrots, red and yellow peppers, and haricots verts (small green beans). For an at-home wedding reception after the ceremony, you can serve something heartier, i.e., more caloric. At this point, the bridesmaids will no longer care if they can fit into their gowns and the men, including the groom, will be so relieved the whole thing is over that they'll be ready to eat, drink, and eat some more.

Whether it's a shower for six close friends or a reception for four hundred, go to whatever length and expense you want to show the bride and groom the best time of their lives, but don't forget the spirit of the football wedding—a little food and a lot of good fellowship wins out over a lot of food and a little good fellowship every time.

Bridal Shower

INSALATA CAPRESE

Mozzarella and Tomato Salad

Serves 8

INGREDIENTS

6 very ripe tomatoes, preferably New Jersey beefsteaks,
   cut into ½-inch-thick slices
1 pound fresh mozzarella or *mozzarella di bufala,*
   cut into the same number of slices as the tomatoes
Salt and freshly ground pepper
¼ cup extra virgin olive oil
Fresh basil leaves for garnish

PREPARATION

Alternate the tomato and mozzarella slices, overlapping slightly on one or two large platters. Sprinkle with salt and pepper. Drizzle with the olive oil. Top with basil leaves.

This salad tastes best when it is not refrigerated—serve it immediately.

49

ITALIAN TUNA SALAD

Serves 4 to 6

INGREDIENTS

1 pound green beans, trimmed

Salt

1 pint cherry or grape tomatoes, halved

3 tender celery ribs, from the center of the bunch

½ small red onion, sliced

¼ cup extra virgin olive oil

2 tablespoons fresh lemon juice

Freshly ground pepper

Two 7-ounce cans imported Italian tuna packed in olive oil

4 hard-cooked eggs, peeled and quartered

Fresh basil or flat-leaf parsley leaves for garnish

PREPARATION

Bring a large pot of water to a boil. Add the green beans and salt to taste and cook until the beans are tender, about 8 minutes. Drain the beans and cool them under cold running water. Drain and pat dry. Cut the beans into bite-sized pieces, and scatter over a large serving platter.

Top the beans with the tomatoes, celery, and onion.

In a small bowl, whisk together the oil, lemon juice, and salt and pepper to taste.

Just before serving, pour the dressing over the vegetables and toss well. Drain the tuna and scatter the chunks over the vegetables. Garnish the platter with the eggs and basil or parsley. Serve immediately.

WATERCRESS AND ORANGE SALAD

Serves 6

INGREDIENTS

2 bunches watercress, rinsed and dried

2 navel oranges, peeled

¼ cup extra virgin olive oil

2 tablespoons fresh lemon juice

Salt and freshly ground pepper

PREPARATION

Remove the tough stems from the watercress and place the leaves in a bowl. You should have about 6 cups.

Cut the oranges into crosswise slices. Cut the slices into bite-sized pieces and place them on top of the watercress.

In a small bowl, whisk together the oil, lemon juice, and salt and pepper to taste. Pour the dressing over the salad and toss well. Serve immediately.

POACHED CHICKEN WITH PESTO

Serves 8 to 12

INGREDIENTS

1 cup packed fresh basil leaves

½ cup packed fresh flat-leaf parsley leaves

1 large garlic clove

2 tablespoons pine nuts

½ cup extra virgin olive oil

Salt

4 cups chicken broth

2 pounds boneless, skinless chicken breasts, trimmed if necessary

Sprigs of fresh basil for garnish

Lemon slices for garnish

PREPARATION

In a food processor or blender, coarsely chop the basil and parsley. Add the garlic and pine nuts and chop fine. With the machine running, slowly add the olive oil. Add salt to taste and blend until smooth. (The pesto sauce can be made ahead. Cover and let stand at room temperature up to 1 hour, or refrigerate overnight. The oil will solidify if chilled; let warm to room temperature and stir well before using.)

In a wide pot or large deep skillet, bring the chicken broth to a simmer. Add the chicken breasts. If they are not covered by the liquid, add a little water. Bring the liquid back to a simmer. Cover and cook for 5 minutes. Turn the chicken breasts and cook 5 minutes more, or until they are just cooked through when cut in the thickest part. Drain the chicken and let cool 5 minutes on a cutting board.

Cut the chicken into crosswise slices. Fan the slices out on a large platter. Drizzle with the sauce. Garnish with basil sprigs and lemon slices, and serve.

ANGINETTI

Lemon Knot Cookies

Makes 3 dozen

INGREDIENTS

4 cups all-purpose flour

3½ teaspoons baking powder

Pinch of salt

1 cup sugar

½ cup solid vegetable shortening

2 teaspoons grated lemon zest

3 large eggs

½ cup milk

2 tablespoons fresh lemon juice

GLAZE

1½ cups confectioners' sugar

1 tablespoon fresh lemon juice

2 teaspoons grated lemon zest

PREPARATION

Sift together the flour, baking powder, and salt onto a piece of wax paper.

In a large mixer bowl, beat together the sugar and shortening until light and fluffy. Beat in the lemon zest, then beat in the eggs one at a time until blended. Beat in the milk and lemon juice, scraping the sides of the bowl. Holding the wax paper like a funnel, add the dry ingredients, mixing until blended. The dough will be soft and sticky. Cover the bowl with plastic wrap. Chill at least 2 hours, or overnight.

Preheat the oven to 350°F. Line two large baking sheets with foil.

Divide the dough into thirds. Cut each third into 12 pieces. Roll one piece between your hands into a 6-inch rope, tie the rope into a loose knot, and place on a baking sheet. Continue with the remaining dough, placing the knots about 1 inch apart.

Bake 12 minutes, or until firm and lightly golden. Let the cookies cool on the pans for 5 minutes. Transfer the cookies to racks to cool completely.

To make the glaze, combine the confectioners' sugar, lemon juice and zest, in a small bowl. Stir in water 1 teaspoon at a time until the glaze is as thick as heavy cream.

Brush the glaze over the tops of the cookies. Place them on racks to dry. Store in an air-tight container in the refrigerator.

BACI CAKE

Chocolate Hazelnut "Kisses" Torte

Serves 8 to 10

INGREDIENTS

8 ounces semisweet chocolate,
  chopped
½ pound (2 sticks) unsalted butter,
  cut into small pieces
1 cup sugar
6 large eggs, separated
2 tablespoons dark rum
1½ cups skinned toasted hazelnuts,
  finely chopped
Pinch of salt

GLAZE

6 ounces bittersweet chocolate,
  chopped
2 tablespoons unsalted butter
2 tablespoons chopped toasted
  hazelnuts for garnish

PREPARATION

Preheat the oven to 350°F. Grease and flour a 9 x 2-inch round cake pan or spring-form pan. Tap out the excess flour.

Put the chocolate in the top of a double boiler or in a heatproof bowl. Place over a pan of simmering water and let stand, uncovered, until the chocolate is softened. Stir until smooth. Remove from the heat. Let cool.

In a large mixer bowl, beat the butter and sugar until light and fluffy, about 3 minutes. Add the egg yolks and rum and beat until smooth. With a rubber spatula, stir in the melted chocolate and hazelnuts.

In another large bowl, with clean beaters, beat the egg whites and salt on medium speed until foamy. Increase the speed to high and beat until soft peaks form when the beaters are lifted.

With a rubber spatula, gently fold a large scoop of the whites into the chocolate mixture to lighten it, then gradually fold in the remainder.

Scrape the batter into the prepared pan. Bake 55 minutes, or until the cake is firm around the edge but still soft in the center. Let the cake cool in the pan on a wire rack for 10 minutes.

Unmold the cake onto the rack. Let the cake cool completely, upside down.

Cut four 2-inch-wide strips of wax paper. Arrange the strips around the edges of the serving plate, to keep the edges clean while you frost the cake. Slide the cake, still upside down, onto the wax paper strips.

To make the glaze, combine the chocolate with the butter in the top of a double boiler or in a heatproof bowl. Place over a pan of simmering water and let stand, uncovered, until the chocolate is softened. Stir until smooth.

Pour the glaze over the cake, letting some spill over the sides. Smooth the sides and top of the cake with a spatula. Sprinkle the hazelnuts over the top of the cake.

Cover with a large overturned bowl, so as not to touch the icing, and refrigerate until 1 hour before serving.

STRAWBERRIES IN ASTI SPUMANTE

Serves 6

INGREDIENTS

1 bottle (750 milliliters) Asti Spumante, well chilled

2 tablespoons crème de cassis

12 to 18 small strawberries, rinsed

PREPARATION

Fill six chilled champagne glasses about two-thirds full with Asti Spumante. Add a teaspoon of crème de cassis to each glass. (Grand Marnier tastes good, too, but it won't give you a pink color.) Float 2 or 3 strawberries in each glass. Serve immediately.

Wedding Reception
CHEESE PUFFS

Makes about 50

INGREDIENTS

1 cup water

8 tablespoons (1 stick) unsalted
   butter, cut into ½-inch pieces

½ teaspoon salt

1 cup all-purpose flour

4 large eggs

1 large egg yolk

1½ cups grated Gruyère

½ cup freshly grated
   Parmigiano-Reggiano

PREPARATION

Preheat the oven to 400°F. Grease two large baking sheets.

Put the water, butter, and salt in a medium heavy saucepan over high heat. Bring to a boil, stirring with a wooden spoon until the butter is melted. Add the flour and cook over medium heat, stirring, until the mixture pulls away from the sides of the pan. Continue to cook and stir for 1 minute more to remove excess moisture from the dough. Remove the pan from the heat.

With a wooden spoon or a hand-held electric mixer on high speed, beat in the eggs and yolk one at a time, beating well after each addition until incorporated. Add the cheeses and beat until blended.

Scoop up a little less than a tablespoon of the mixture, and use a second spoon to push the batter onto one of the baking sheets. Continue making small mounds, placing them about 2 inches apart so that they have room to expand. Dip your finger into cold water and pat the mounds to round the tops. (You can make these up to 24 hours ahead of time. Cover them loosely with foil and refrigerate until ready to bake.)

Bake 18 to 20 minutes, or until golden brown and crisp. Serve warm, or transfer the puffs to a rack and let cool.

To store, place the puffs in tightly sealed plastic bags and refrigerate up to 2 days, or freeze up to 1 month. Reheat them on a baking sheet in a 350°F oven, without thawing if frozen.

59

CANNELLONI

Serves 12

INGREDIENTS

Béchamel Sauce (page 101)

1 cup freshly grated
  Parmigiano-Reggiano

FILLING

1 pound ground veal

8 ounces Italian-style pork sausage,
  casings removed

1 large garlic clove, minced

Two 10-ounce packages frozen chopped
  spinach, cooked, drained,
  and squeezed dry

Salt and freshly ground pepper

TO ASSEMBLE

1½ pounds homemade or
  store-bought fresh pasta,
  such as fresh lasagne sheets,
  cut into 4-inch squares

½ cup freshly grated
  Parmigiano-Reggiano

PREPARATION

Prepare the béchamel and set aside. To make the filling, heat a large skillet over medium heat. Add the meats and garlic and cook, stirring frequently with a wooden spoon, until the meat is no longer pink. Tip the pan and spoon off the excess fat. Stir in the spinach and 1 cup of the béchamel sauce. Taste for salt and pepper. If the sausage is highly seasoned, you may not need any. Remove from the heat and let cool slightly, then stir in the cheese.

Bring a large pot of water to a boil and add salt to taste. Have ready a large bowl of cold water, and spread out some lint-free (not terry cloth) kitchen towels on a flat surface.

Add the pasta squares to the pot a few at a time and cook less than 1 minute; they should be slightly underdone. Scoop the pasta out of the pot and place it in the cold water until cool enough to handle, then lay the pasta squares out flat on the towels. Continue cooking and cooling the remaining pasta in the same way.

Preheat the oven to 350°F. Butter two 11 x 8 x 2-inch baking dishes.

To assemble the cannelloni, spread a thin layer of sauce over the bottom of each baking dish.

Spread some of the filling over each pasta square, leaving a ½-inch border along one side. Starting at the opposite side, loosely roll up each pasta square, and place the rolls seam side down in the baking dishes. Spoon the remaining sauce over the pasta. Sprinkle with the cheese. (The cannelloni can be assembled up to 1 day ahead. Cover with plastic wrap and refrigerate.)

Bake 30 minutes (longer if the dish has been refrigerated), or until the sauce is bubbling and the top is golden brown. Serve hot.

ROASTED BEEF TENDERLOIN

Serves 12

INGREDIENTS

Two 3- to 3½-pound trimmed and tied center-cut beef tenderloin roasts

3 tablespoons olive oil

1 teaspoon dried thyme

1 teaspoon salt

1 teaspoon coarsely ground black pepper

PREPARATION

Preheat the oven to 425°F. Oil a large roasting pan.

Pat the beef dry with paper towels.

Mix together the oil, thyme, salt, and pepper. Rub the meat all over with the mixture.

Place the beef in the pan. Roast 30 minutes, or until the temperature on an instant-read thermometer inserted in the center reads 120°F for rare. Remove the meat to a cutting board and let stand, loosely covered with foil, for 15 minutes. (The meat will continue to cook and the temperature will rise about 10 degrees, reaching 130°F for medium-rare.)

Cut the meat into ½-inch slices and arrange them on a platter. Serve hot or at room temperature.

ROASTED POTATOES WITH ROSEMARY AND GARLIC

Serves 12

INGREDIENTS

4 pounds small (1½ inch wide) boiling potatoes, such as Yukon Gold,
   peeled and halved

⅓ cup olive oil

3 tablespoons chopped fresh rosemary

Salt and freshly ground pepper

2 large garlic cloves, thinly sliced

PREPARATION

Preheat the oven to 400°F.

Pat the potato pieces dry with paper towels. In one or two baking pans large enough
to hold them in a single layer, toss the potatoes with the oil, rosemary, and salt and
pepper to taste.

Roast the potatoes for 30 minutes.

Add the garlic and stir the potatoes. Roast 20 to 30 minutes more, or until the potatoes are browned and tender. Serve hot.

STUFFED MUSHROOMS

Serves 12

INGREDIENTS

36 large cremini or white mushrooms (about 2½ pounds)

1½ cups plain dry bread crumbs, preferably homemade from Italian bread

½ cup freshly grated Parmigiano-Reggiano

2 garlic cloves, minced

½ cup chopped fresh flat-leaf parsley

Salt and freshly ground pepper

½ cup olive oil

PREPARATION

Preheat the oven to 400°F. Oil one or two baking pans large enough to hold the mushrooms in a single layer.

Wash the mushrooms quickly under running water and pat dry. (Don't let them soak, or they will become waterlogged.) Snap off the stems and set them aside.

Arrange the mushroom caps upside down in the prepared pans.

Trim off the ends of the stems. Chop the stems and place them in a bowl. Add the bread crumbs, cheese, garlic, parsley, and salt and pepper to taste. Stir in the oil.

Spoon the crumb mixture into the mushroom caps.

Bake the mushrooms 18 to 20 minutes, or until tender. Serve hot.

ASPARAGUS WITH LEMON

Serves 12

INGREDIENTS

2½ pounds asparagus, trimmed

Salt

⅔ cup extra virgin olive oil

2 to 3 tablespoons fresh lemon juice

Freshly ground pepper

PREPARATION

Bring about 2 inches of water to a boil in a large skillet. Add half the asparagus and salt to taste. Cook until the asparagus bend slightly when you lift them from the stem end, about 5 to 8 minutes, depending on thickness. Remove the asparagus with a slotted spatula, rinse them under cold water, and set aside. Cook the remaining asparagus in the same way.

Pat the asparagus dry and arrange on a platter. They can stand at room temperature up to 3 hours.

In a small bowl, whisk together the oil, lemon juice, and salt and pepper to taste. Drizzle the dressing over the asparagus and serve immediately.

ROASTED CHERRY TOMATOES WITH BASIL

Serves 12

INGREDIENTS

3 pints cherry or grape tomatoes
¼ cup olive oil
Salt and freshly ground pepper
2 tablespoons chopped fresh basil

PREPARATION

Preheat the oven to 425°F.

In a large shallow roasting pan, toss the tomatoes with the oil and salt and pepper to taste.

Roast the tomatoes 8 to 10 minutes, or until the skins begin to split. Remove the tomatoes to a serving bowl and sprinkle with the basil. Serve hot.

VENETIANS

Rainbow Cookies

Makes 6 dozen

INGREDIENTS

One 8-ounce can almond paste

¾ pound (3 sticks) unsalted butter, cut into small pieces

1 cup sugar

4 large eggs, separated

¼ teaspoon salt

2 cups all-purpose flour

6 drops red food coloring, or to desired color

6 drops green food coloring, or to desired color

1 cup seedless raspberry jam

8 ounces semisweet or bittersweet chocolate, chopped

PREPARATION

Preheat the oven to 350°F. Butter three 13 x 9 x 2-inch baking pans. Line the pans with wax paper and butter the paper.

Crumble the almond paste into a large mixer bowl. Add the butter, ½ cup of the sugar, the egg yolks, and salt. Beat until light and fluffy. Beat in the flour just until blended.

In another large bowl, with clean beaters, beat the egg whites on medium speed until foamy. Gradually beat in the remaining ½ cup sugar. Beat on high speed until the egg whites form soft peaks when the beaters are lifted.

With a rubber spatula, fold one-third of the whites into the yolk mixture to lighten it. Gradually fold in the remaining whites.

Scoop out ⅓ of the batter and spread it evenly in one of the pans. It will be about ¼ inch thick. Bake 10 to 12 minutes, or until the cake is just set and very lightly colored around the edges.

Meanwhile, scoop half of the remaining batter into another bowl. Fold the red food coloring into one bowl of batter and the green into the other. Spread the batter in the two remaining pans and bake as for the first layer. Let the cake layers cool in the pans for 5 minutes.

Transfer the cake layers to cooling racks, leaving the wax paper attached. Let cool completely.

Using the wax paper to lift it, place the green layer paper side up on a tray. Carefully peel off the paper. Spread the cake with half of the jam. Place the white layer paper side up on top of the first. Peel off the paper and spread the cake with the remaining jam. Place the red layer paper side up on top. Peel off the paper.

Wrap the cake in foil or plastic wrap. Place a weight such as a cutting board on top to compact the layers. Refrigerate the cake at least 1 hour, or overnight.

Place the chocolate in the top of a double boiler or in a small heatproof bowl. Place over a pan of simmering water and let stand, uncovered, until the chocolate is softened. Stir until smooth. Remove from the heat.

Remove the weight and unwrap the cake. Pour the melted chocolate onto the cake and spread it smoothly over the top with a spatula, leaving the sides uncovered.

Refrigerate 30 minutes, or until the chocolate is lightly set. (Sometimes these are called 7-Layer Cookies. These have only six layers, but if you want to make a seventh, let the chocolate set until firm. Turn the whole cake upside down and spread the bottom with additional melted chocolate. Chill until set.)

Using a ruler as a guide, cut the cake into 1½ x 1-inch rectangles. Store the cookies in an airtight container in the refrigerator.

Chapter 4

Come to My Home:
Open Houses and Family Reunions

I love big, informal parties. From early on in our marriage, when we still lived in a second-story walk-up in West Orange, New Jersey, my husband and I have thrown an open house party for our friends and family almost yearly. At first the "planning" consisted of, "You bring the cheap wine, we'll make sandwiches and buy the gelato." As we moved up in the world, this free-form affair became more elaborate but nevertheless relaxed and free-spirited. The great thing about a get-together like this is that there are no expectations—no speeches, no formal dining requirements, no obligatory envelopes of cash or toaster ovens. The only obligation of the guest is just to show up in a good spirit. The rest is up to the host.

Assuming you are willing to take the plunge and invite a slew of people over to your house for no particular reason, your first decision is simple—indoors or out? Given that we now have a nice big backyard with a pool and Jacuzzi, I inevitably choose outdoors, which also means that guests will wander throughout the house anyway. I guess this is the 1950s suburban model of the house party, as opposed to an urban apartment or condo party. First, some thoughts on this kind of indoor affair: I think if I lived in a city apartment or some other place without a big yard

for entertaining, I'd give a lot more thought to a party design that was casual but slightly more stylish than an outdoor barbecue and swim. A color scheme I'd love to try in this setting is basic white with cocoa brown and light blue touches: for instance, simple white plates and stemware on a dark brown tablecloth with matching napkins. Any white or light blue floral arrangement—a row of potted white orchids, say, or white apple blossoms branches in a vase—would be an elegant contrast.

sore. You might also rent a big party tent, just for the fun of it. If it rains, you're home free. If it's broiling, your guests will kiss your hand. A big tent is also a way of focusing the party if your backyard is mostly undefined open space. Plant the buffet table and bar and/or folding tables and chairs under the tent, and you'll feel like you're throwing an elegant fete on your summer estate—even if your "estate" is a suburban plot and the dining motif is paper and plastic.

Come on Over!

Sopranos' Annual
Open House

Saturday, May 19th
North Caldwell, N.J.

I would opt for this every time—colorful, sturdy, but disposable paper or plastic plates, glasses and silverware, or some throwaway variation that you come across at the discount store. If you don't like paper napkins, try small, inexpensive dish towels. If you use a lightweight tablecloth, here's a little tip: Weigh down the corners with metal washers you pick up at the hardware store. Use a seam ripper to discreetly open the cloth hem a few inches, then

The affair would be a buffet and people would sit or stand where they pleased. I think of open houses as warm-weather events, so even if you are indoors, if the temperature is not in the nineties, think of opening the windows and doors and letting the outside in.

For our outdoor affairs, I always send invitations with something catchy on the cover. One year I had then-eight-year-old AJ hand draw a picture of our house, then copied it for the invite. When entertaining outside, think of your backyard as a big, grassy living room. Besides cleaning the place up, don't reject the idea of renting a few large plants or shrubs to fill out your landscape design or hide some eye-

insert the washers.

Just because you are outside doesn't mean you shouldn't add flowers to the mix. You may not have sunflowers or daisies in your garden, but there is no reason you can't have big bunches of them on the buffet table or scattered around the pool. The bird of paradise flower, commonplace in California and Arizona, looks daring and exotic in a New Jersey backyard. Trust me.

If people, i.e., kids, are swimming as well as dining at your open house, be extremely safety minded. Pool drowning is a leading cause of death among small children in America, and a third of those deaths occur in the pool of a friend or relative.

HOW TO LOOK GOOD IN FAMILY SNAPSHOTS

A local party photographer gave me these wonderful pointers on how to look your best for family photos, large and small. Pay attention. These hints could save you years of grimacing as you flip through the scrapbook.

- Don't face the camera head-on. Turn slightly sideways. Both your face and torso will look thinner, if that's your concern. Pose so that one-third of your face is slyly turned away from the camera.

- Look up at the camera, not down. Looking down will give you a double chin. Make sure the photographer is either at your eye level or slightly above.

- If you are worried about a fleshy neck, project your chin outwards. If you pull your head in, your neck and head meet. If you push it out a little, your neck magically becomes longer and more slender. Stand straight while doing this, of course.

- If it's a solo shot, stand near a window or a pool of water so that light can bounce off part of your face. This creates a nice, luminous effect and hides wrinkles.

- V-necks are better than turtlenecks or round-necked apparel. Solid colors are better than patterns. Flashy patterns might make you the center of the photo, but maybe not in the way you wanted.

- Are your eyes always closed in photos? Keep them closed, have the photographer count to three, then open them. Works every time.

- Smiling on cue is extremely hard for some people. I know of no magic solution to this problem. You can either convince yourself to smile or not. To avoid a manufactured smile, you might try to think of something that genuinely pleases you. Maybe it's a photo of yourself with a natural smile!

- When in doubt about how you look or feel, stand in the back row.

Meadow Soprano – "My Grandmother Couldn't Cook."
Sociology 411: "Ethnic American Studies"

Page 2

Her inability to cook and reward her family with the loving sustenance of good food, a cultural tradition in the Italian community going back hundreds if not thousands of years, marked her children for life. One daughter clearly has eating issues to this day. I've watched her at the dinner table loudly complaining that she wasn't getting "her share" while her plate was overflowing with pasta, vegetables, and even an early glob of dessert. Another daughter eats like a bird, as if she were still afraid that her mother might poison her with a charred-black roast or a three-day-old fish. One expresses constant need, the other, constant revulsion—same mother, two different wounds.

The one son in this dysfunctional clan loves food but may have a deeper mother-induced neurosis than even his two sisters. Before she passed away, he had a very volatile relationship with his mother and often accused her of selfishness and greed. Maybe, foodwise, she took the best cut of meat for herself and gave her son the fatty portion. He also has had periodic fainting spells that may be food-related, or at least refrigerator-related. I can't say more without revealing some family secrets.

In conclusion, food and love in the Italian-American culture are deeply, inextricably interconnected.

Meadow –
Intriguing assessment. How does
your family's history influence your
views on food?

A-

Designate someone to be the pool watcher at
all times and give him or her a half-in-jest
tank top reading "Lifeguard." Having that
person in place, turn the pool into a game
room. Water pistols, beach balls, rafts, pool
basketball, or volleyball—load up on these
distractions. And assume your guests,
swimming and sitting, will have forgotten
towels, sunscreen, bug spray, and hats or
parasols to avoid the sun—go to an import
store and buy a dozen cheap paper or cloth
parasols. They'll be used and appreciated.

One last item to consider: sand. You
can go all out and have a truckload of sand
delivered and plopped down by the pool
for kids to play in. Or you could just fill small buck-
ets full of sand and stick flowers, candles, or
seashells in them. Seashells also make excellent

WINE SUGGESTIONS

Fiano di Avellino
{ a white wine from Campania, specifically
from Avellino, my husband's homeland }

Nero d'Avola
{ a red wine from Sicily,
my mother's homeland }

Moscato di Pontelleria
{ a Sicilian dessert wine }

THE OUT-OF-CONTROL GUEST
by Bobby Bacala

Nothing ruins a party faster than one or two loud, inebriated, possibly hostile guests who might have a serious drinking problem or just be facing a personal crisis or disappointment of some kind, you don't know. My own three-step plan for dealing with such a troublemaker is simple: Designate. Delubricate. Isolate.

First, designate someone at the party to watch over Mr. Lampshade. If you do this job yourself, you won't have time to host, and the party will suffer. The first thing this handler should do is confiscate the person's car keys. He or she should also engage said drunk in friendly chatter, lead them to the food table, etc., i.e., anything to keep them from drinking more. The handler shouldn't be snide, sarcastic, or start an argument—this could set your friend off and make a bad situation even worse.

To delubricate, water is good, very good, but coffee, contrary to popular myth, often isn't. The caffeine will keep him awake, but coffee, like alcohol, dehydrates and thus doesn't help the alcohol move through the system. Soft drinks are worth a try, if they keep the guy happy.

If all else fails, isolate. You don't want the guy driving home, so unless someone else, say, an embarrassed spouse or girlfriend, is willing to pour him into a car, lead him into isolation. A spare bedroom is a retreat, or a spare bathroom, if you have one. Outside by the patio is good too. Fresh air, along with a gallon or two of water, might just unslosh his pickled brain. Don't let him wander into the pool, though. This could be tragic.

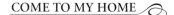

Mangiamo!

Even if you know some basic Italian-American food terms like *"gabagool"* (capicola) or "Sunday gravy" (tomato sauce with meat), other expressions heard at your favorite Italian restaurant might throw you. They're easy to pick up though; for your next Italian-themed celebration, try sprinkling the meal with a few of them.

Mangiamo! – Let's eat! Also heard: *Mangia! Mangia!* – Eat! Eat!

Benvenuto! – Welcome! If it's more than one person at the door, *"Benvenuti!"* The whole phrase would be *"Benvenuti a casa mia,"* or "Welcome to my home."

Googootz – a very long, pale green summer squash. Also used for zucchini or a dish using zucchini. Just a fun word to throw around.

Mordevahm (*morte di fame*) – someone who makes a pig of themselves, a glutton, a hog, as in, "Don't invite Cousin Al. He's a *mordevahm.*"

Skeeve (*schifo*) – as a noun, a disgusting person, like the *mordevahm.*

Gavone – a person who always does the wrong thing, a jerk, i.e., the kind of difficult guest you wished you hadn't invited to the party.

Moppeen' (*mappina*) – dish towel. If you're not a *skeeve* or a *gavone*, you'll offer to pick one up at a big, informal affair like an open house.

Grazie – Thank you. Someone sticks a plate of pasta in front of you, you say, *"Grazie. Grazie."*

throwaway ashtrays. The farther away from the beach you live, the more novel creating a beach in your backyard becomes.

A family reunion, at least to my mind, should be much the same kind of open, informal affair, except the guest list is limited to whoever fits the definition of "family." If people must come from a long distance and be entertained for more than a day, then you are faced with a spiral notebook full of problems not addressed here. But if you are lucky like I am, and a reunion of your family demands that no one drives on an interstate for more than an hour, then the open-house model fits. For a reunion, throw in a party favor commemorating the event, like a baseball hat or a T-shirt printed with the family name. One more thing to add to a family gathering are mementos of the past: photo albums, 8mm film reels, home videos of the generation now passed. At these kinds of events, the past is the tie that binds and brings fractious in-laws together, if only for the group shot at the end of the party.

Some social rituals are built-in—baptisms, holidays, birthdays, wakes. Some are just made up

and become rituals only because someone, i.e., you, decides to make them an annual occurrence and you are willing to throw yourself, and your home, into the yearly act of giving dozens of friends and relatives a good time. To quote a phrase I learned from Dr. Melfi, open houses like this grow out of a simple human instinct: the "urge to merge." Unless you are a hermit, a wallflower, or simply a person who hates people, you know exactly what I mean. Go ahead, throw one house party. It might become "your thing."

prosecco bellini

Combine 1 part fresh peach puree to 3 parts chilled Prosecco, an Italian sparkling white wine. Serve in a champagne flute and garnish with a fresh peach slice. To serve a dozen or so guests, combine 1 quart fresh peach puree, 3 quarts chilled Prosecco, and 1 tablespoon fresh lemon juice in a punch bowl. Add fresh peach slices.

bloody mary

Combine 6 ounces cold tomato juice, 1/4 teaspoon Worcestershire sauce, 1 1/2 ounces vodka, 1 teaspoon fresh lemon juice, several dashes Tabasco sauce, several pinches of celery salt, and a pinch of white pepper. Serve in a chilled Collins glass and garnish with a celery stalk.

CHEESE

A few quick pointers on Italian cheese:

For grating and cooking, the best cheeses are Parmesan and Pecorino Romano. The finest Italian Parmesan is known by its real name, Parmigiano Reggiano. It doesn't come pre-grated in a can and it is expensive, but it's worth it for the intense flavor. Made from cow's milk, it tastes rich and nutty and is especially good with cream or butter sauces on pasta and vegetables. Or just eat it plain as a snack.

Pecorino Romano is made from sheep's milk and is sharper and saltier than Parmesan. Use it when you want a tangier cheese flavor. It works well in tomato sauces, vegetable sauces, and those made with garlic and olive oil. Don't confuse it with "romano," a bland cheese made from cow's milk. Some people ask for Locatelli, which is just a brand name for Pecorino Romano, one of many.

Always buy the cheese in a whole piece, never grated. Grated cheese dries out quickly and loses its flavor. A whole piece will keep in the fridge for a long time. To grate it, use an old-fashioned box grater, a hand-cranked drum grater, or a cheese rasp. Or, if you need a lot of grated cheese, stick it in a food processor.

Sprinkle cheese on most pasta dishes to enhance the flavor, but never on pasta with fish, like spaghetti with clams. The cheese overwhelms the flavor of the fish.

CARMELA'S LASAGNE WITH BASIL LEAVES

Serves 8 to 10

INGREDIENTS

1 pound dried lasagne

5 to 6 cups Meat Sauce (page 82)

2 pounds ricotta

Salt and freshly ground pepper

1 cup freshly grated Parmigiano-Reggiano or Pecorino Romano

1 large bunch basil, leaves removed, rinsed, and dried

12 ounces fresh mozzarella, thinly sliced

PREPARATION

In a large pot, bring at least 4 quarts salted water to a boil. Add a few pieces of lasagne and cook, stirring gently, until tender but slightly underdone. Scoop the pasta out of the water with a sieve, and cool it in a bowl of cold water. Cook the remaining pasta the same way. When cool enough to handle, lay the lasagne out flat on lint-free (not terry cloth) kitchen towels. The towels can be stacked.

In a bowl, beat the ricotta and salt and pepper to taste.

Spread a thin layer of the sauce in a 13 x 9 x 2-inch baking pan. Place a few sheets of lasagne in the pan in a single layer, overlapping them slightly. Spread evenly with about one-third of the ricotta mixture and sprinkle with 2 tablespoons of the grated cheese. Make a layer of basil leaves and another of mozzarella slices on top. Make two more layers the same way. Top with a final layer of lasagne, sauce, and the remaining grated cheese. (The lasagne can be made ahead to this point. Cover with plastic wrap and refrigerate several hours, or overnight.)

Place a rack in the center of the oven. Preheat the oven to 375°F.

Bake the lasagne for 45 minutes. If the lasagne is browning too much, cover it loosely with foil. Bake 15 minutes more (longer if it has been refrigerated), or until the top is browned and the sauce is bubbling around the edges. Let stand 15 minutes.

Cut the lasagne into squares and serve.

MEAT SAUCE

Makes about 8 cups

INGREDIENTS

1 medium onion, chopped

3 large garlic cloves, chopped

2 tablespoons olive oil

8 ounces sweet Italian-style sausage, casings removed

1 pound ground beef sirloin

Salt and freshly ground pepper

One 35-ounce can Italian peeled tomatoes, chopped

One 28-ounce can tomato puree

6 fresh basil leaves, torn into bits

PREPARATION

In a large saucepan, cook the onion and garlic in the oil over medium heat, stirring occasionally, until softened, about 7 minutes.

Stir in the sausage meat, breaking up the lumps with the back of a spoon. Add the beef and salt and pepper to taste. Cook, stirring often, until the meat is nicely browned and crumbly. Tip the pan; if there is a lot of fat, spoon some of it out and discard it.

Add the tomatoes and tomato puree, then add about ½ cup water to each can and swirl it around to rinse out the can. Add the liquid to the pan, along with salt and pepper to taste. Partially cover the pan and bring the sauce to a simmer. Reduce the heat to low and cook, stirring occasionally, until the sauce is thickened and the oil has separated from the tomatoes, about 1½ hours.

Stir in the basil and cook 5 minutes more.

Serve immediately, or let cool, cover, and refrigerate up to 3 days. This sauce also freezes well.

POTATO PIE

Serves 8 to 10

INGREDIENTS

3 pounds boiling potatoes, peeled and quartered

1 cup warm milk

6 tablespoons unsalted butter, melted

½ cup plus 2 tablespoons freshly grated Pecorino Romano

2 large eggs, beaten

Salt and freshly ground pepper

4 ounces fresh mozzarella, chopped

4 ounces smoked mozzarella (or substitute more fresh mozzarella), chopped

4 ounces sliced prosciutto or salami, chopped

PREPARATION

Place the potatoes in a large saucepan with cold water to cover. Cover and bring to a boil. Boil gently over medium-low heat until the potatoes are tender when pierced with a sharp knife, about 20 minutes. Drain and transfer to a large bowl. Let cool slightly.

Preheat the oven to 400°F. Butter a 2½-quart baking dish.

Mash the potatoes thoroughly with a potato masher. Stir in the milk, butter, ½ cup of the grated cheese, the eggs, and salt and pepper to taste. Add the mozzarella and prosciutto and mix well. Scrape the mixture into the prepared dish and smooth the top. Sprinkle with the remaining 2 tablespoons grated cheese.

Bake 45 to 50 minutes, or until browned around the edges. Let cool 15 minutes before serving.

POLPETTONE

Stuffed Meat Loaf

Serves 6 to 8

INGREDIENTS

4 slices day-old Italian bread, crusts removed

½ cup milk

1 pound ground beef sirloin

½ pound ground pork

1 garlic clove, finely chopped

1 large egg, beaten

½ cup freshly grated Parmigiano-Reggiano

¼ cup chopped fresh flat-leaf parsley

1 teaspoon salt

Freshly ground pepper

STUFFING

3 ounces sliced prosciutto or mortadella

3 ounces provolone, chopped

3 hard-cooked eggs, peeled

PREPARATION

Preheat the oven to 350°F. Oil a 13 x 9 x 2-inch baking pan.

Tear the bread into small pieces. You should have about 1 cup. Soak the bread in the milk until it is soft, then gently squeeze out the excess milk.

In a large bowl, combine the soaked bread, beef, pork, garlic, beaten egg, grated cheese, parsley, salt, and pepper to taste. Mix well with your hands.

Sprinkle a large sheet of wax paper or parchment with water. Pat the meat mixture out to form a rectangle about ½ inch thick. Arrange the prosciutto slices on top of the meat. Scatter the provolone on

top of the prosciutto. Arrange the hard-cooked eggs in a row lengthwise down the center.

Lift one long side of the paper and carefully roll up the meat, enclosing the filling and peeling off the paper as you go. Pinch the ends of the meat roll closed to seal in the filling. Transfer the roll to the prepared pan, seam side down.

Bake 1 hour and 10 minutes, or until the internal temperature of the loaf reaches 155°F on an instant-read thermometer. Let cool at least 10 minutes before slicing.

Serve hot or at room temperature. If you like, serve with Tomato Sauce (page 32).

ARUGULA AND MUSHROOM SALAD

Serves 6

INGREDIENTS

2 large bunches arugula, trimmed, washed, and dried

¼ cup extra virgin olive oil

2 tablespoons fresh lemon juice

1 teaspoon Dijon mustard

Salt and freshly ground pepper

4 ounces white mushrooms, very thinly sliced

PREPARATION

Tear the arugula leaves into bite-sized pieces. You should have about 6 cups.

In a jar, combine the oil, lemon juice, mustard, and salt and pepper to taste. Shake until well blended.

Just before serving, toss the arugula and mushrooms with the dressing.

GREEN BEANS IN TOMATO SAUCE

Serves 4

INGREDIENTS

2 garlic cloves, fincly chopped

¼ cup olive oil

1½ cups canned Italian peeled tomatoes, with their juice

1 pound green beans, trimmed

Salt and freshly ground pepper

½ cup fresh basil leaves

PREPARATION

In a large skillet, cook the garlic in the olive oil over medium heat until lightly golden, about 2 minutes. Add the tomatoes and chop them coarsely with the side of a spoon. Bring to a simmer and cook 5 minutes.

Add the green beans and salt and pepper to taste. Cover the pan and cook, stirring occasionally, until the beans are tender, about 8 minutes. Stir in the basil.

Transfer the beans and sauce to a serving bowl. Or, if there is a lot of liquid left in the pan, remove the beans to a serving bowl, raise the heat, and boil the sauce until thickened. Pour the sauce over the beans and serve.

PASTICIOTTI

Little Vanilla Cream Tartlets

Serves 6

INGREDIENTS

PASTRY CREAM FILLING

1 cup milk

2 large egg yolks

⅓ cup sugar

2 tablespoons all-purpose flour

1 teaspoon pure vanilla extract

CRUST

3¼ cups all purpose flour

½ cup sugar

2 teaspoons baking powder

1 teaspoon salt

½ pound (2 sticks) unsalted butter

2 large eggs, lightly beaten

1 cup milk

2 teaspoons pure vanilla extract

1 egg yolk, beaten with 1
  tablespoon water

Confectioners' sugar

PREPARATION

To make the filling, heat the milk in a medium saucepan over low heat until bubbles form around the edges. Remove from the heat.

In a medium bowl, whisk the egg yolks and sugar until pale yellow. Whisk in the flour. Gradually add the hot milk, whisking constantly. Transfer the mixture to the saucepan and cook over medium heat, stirring constantly, until boiling. Reduce the heat and simmer for 1 minute, or until the mixture is thick and coats the back of the spoon. Scrape the mixture into a bowl and stir in the vanilla. Place a piece of plastic wrap directly on the surface of the cream to prevent a skin from forming. Let cool slightly, then refrigerate at least several hours, or overnight, until cold.

To make the crust, in a large mixer bowl or a food processor, stir or pulse together the flour, sugar, baking powder, and salt. Add the butter and blend, mix, or pulse until it is the size of small peas.

Beat together the eggs, milk, and vanilla. Add the liquid to the dry ingredients and mix or pulse just until the dough comes together. Add a little ice water if it seems dry and crumbly.

Gather the dough into a ball. Cut the dough into 2 pieces, one slightly larger than the other. Shape the pieces into disks, and wrap each piece in plastic wrap. Refrigerate at least 1 hour, or overnight.

Preheat the oven to 350°F. Grease eight 2½ x ½-inch tartlet pans.

On a floured surface, roll out the dough to a ¼-inch thickness. This dough is very soft, so keep it well chilled. Cut the dough into 8 circles 1½ inches wider than the pans. Line the pans with the dough, pressing it gently into the bottom and up the sides; patch it with scraps of dough if it tears. Fill the tart shells about three-quarters full with the pastry cream. Don't overfill them, or the cream will leak out when the tarts are baked.

Roll out the remaining dough to about ¼ inch thickness. Cut out circles slightly larger than the tops of the pans. Place the circles on top of the tarts. Seal the edges by pressing with a fork.

Brush the tops with the egg mixture. With a small knife, cut 4 slits in the top of each tart.

Bake 30 to 40 minutes, or until golden brown. Let the tarts cool in the tins on a rack.

Insert the tip of a small knife between the crust and the pan, to loosen each tart. Slide the tarts onto a plate. Dust with confectioners' sugar before serving. Store in the refrigerator.

Chapter 5

DINNER FOR TWELVE

There are very small dinner parties with a few select friends and there are big open-house–style dinner parties where the guest list includes friends of friends and the mood is carefree. For many, it's the dinner party in the middle that can cause the greatest amount of what Dr. Melfi earlier called "party anxiety." This adults-only affair can involve eight, twelve, or even sixteen and usually means a semi-formal, sit-down format. It's often a party where you invite guests who don't know each other well in an attempt to create a different, hopefully stimulating, new social mix. It is also an occasion to invite people not even you know that well to expand your social circle beyond your small group of old friends. Because there are always unknowable results when you bring new people together for the first time, the party giver often feels the additional burden of playing social director, if not group therapist, as well as hostess and meal server.

If there are enough people and enough food, it's hard to have a disastrous open house. However, disastrous dinner parties for twelve are, unfortunately, all too common. Even so, with the right spirit and a little judicious planning, yours can be a smash.

Let's imagine the perfect dinner party for twelve and work

back from there. Besides you and your spouse, you've invited five other couples, three you've known forever and two you just met recently at a church fundraiser. The two new couples are themselves close friends, which is why you invited them both; neither will feel like the odd man out, so to speak. Just from your brief encounter at the church, you feel the new people could become close friends in time, or at least the two wives and you could. The three of you share an interest in antiquing, say, an interest you'd like to get your old friends into as well. As you're planning the party, you imagine a future

trip to Pennsylvania Dutch country with some or all of the dinner guests to look for antiques. There is so much you can learn about antiques and related topics like interior decorating, gardening, and even real-estate investment from your new friends. They are much more experienced in these areas than you are.

HOW TO SET A TABLE

I did not know this until my friend Charmaine told me the specifics. Maybe you've already learned this somewhere or maybe you could care less where the salad fork goes, but some things are just good to know and this is one of them.

Plates: The main plate—either the entrée dinner plate or a plate that goes under that plate, called a "charger" plate—should be one and a half inches from the table's edge. If there's a salad plate, put it on top of the dinner plate. If there's a soup bowl, put it on top of the salad plate. The bread plate goes to the upper left of the dinner plate.

Silverware: Place it one inch from the table's edge, forks to the left of plate, knife and spoons to the right. One exception: a shellfish fork goes on the right, for whatever reason. The correct order is, from left to right: salad fork, dinner fork, PLATE. Then: salad knife, soup spoon. Blades of knives go in. If there's a bread knife, put it across the bread plate, blade down. A dessert fork goes above the plate, tines facing right. A dessert spoon goes above the fork, bowl facing left.

Glassware: Place a water glass to the right of the dinner plate, directly above the dinner knife. Wineglasses go to the right of the water glass in the order they'll be used. A champagne flute goes behind the wineglasses. Cups and saucers are not part of the main setting. Bring them to the table with dessert.

Napkins: Don't put them under any of the silverware. Place on the salad plate or soup bowl or to the left of the farthest fork.

classic martini

Spear 2 pitted green olives and pla[ce] them in a shot glass with 1½ teaspo[ons] dry vermouth. Combine 1½ cups cracked ice and 3 ounces gin in a cocktail shaker. Shake gently. Set th[e] speared olives in a martini glass. Strain the gin over the olives.

cosmopolitan

Combine 6 ice cubes, 1½ ounces vo[dka,] ½ ounce Triple Sec, 1 teaspoon fres[h] lime juice, 2 teaspoons fresh lemon juice, 1½ teaspoons sugar syrup, and a splash of cranberry juice in a cocktail shaker. Shake, then strain i[nto] a martini glass. Add a squeeze of lim[e] and a lime wedge.

IT'S ALL ABOUT THE TIMING

by Charmaine Bucco, Co-owner, Nuovo Vesuvio Ristorante, Essex County, N.J.

I am a professional restaurateur and caterer and I can tell you from years of experience, planning and timing are everything in pulling off a successful dinner party. You are, in essence, the producer of the party, in the same way someone produces a play or a movie. Don't obsess, but don't count on throwing things together at the last minute: a) you'll forget something vital, and b) you'll be so frazzled, you will probably get drunk and fall asleep during the first course.

Here's the way I would plan a dinner for twelve.

- THREE WEEKS AHEAD. Design and mail invitations. Take inventory of glassware, silverware, china, and tablecloths, i.e., anything you know you'll need for the party. This is not busy work. This is just common sense if you are shooting for anything more than take-out Chinese on paper plates.

- TWO WEEKS AHEAD. Get stuff out of the way, even it seems way too early. Write out place and/or menu cards. Order flowers for a pickup date. Buy wine and liquor, launder tablecloths and napkins, and do a big house clean.

- DAY BEFORE. Hopefully, a small house clean. Pick up flowers and buy all groceries. If vegetables need washing, do it now.

- MORNING OF. Set table, do one last house check for dust and clutter, and prepare anything (see Panna Cotta recipe, following) that can be refrigerated—and check off the food list.

- TWO HOURS BEFORE. Arrange flowers. Prepare main dishes for meal, to be kept warm, if possible, or to be finished by help in the kitchen.

- HALF AN HOUR BEFORE. Everything should be ready except you. Take a shower, relax for minute, get dressed, and take a deep breath or two. Then light the candles, turn on music, if desired, and be ready to have a great time.

The problem is—and this is often the problem in making new adult friends—the husbands have less in common than the wives. Your husband and his two old friends, say, are sports fanatics, while the two new men are investment bankers who travel the world and speak multiple languages. You can't imagine your husband's pals talking about international exchange rates, and you can't imagine the two bankers all that bothered by the Yankees' pitching problems. You see a disaster in the making—what if these men are on opposite sides of the gun-control

issue? What if your husband's friends think the bankers are corporate crooks and the bankers think his friends are dull and uninformed? "What were you thinking?" you might ask yourself halfway through the meal. "These guys hate each other!"

Remember, this is an ideal dinner party, mainly because you will make it so. First of all, don't assume that because people come from different walks of life, they don't have things in common or aren't curious about one another. For instance, one of the bankers might speak Italian, just like your husband's friends. There's an instant bond right there. It'll take them all of five minutes to begin to exchange inappropriate jokes in Italiano. Or maybe one of the bankers' wives, being that her husband is in Europe all the time, watches every Yankee game on cable and actually met Joe DiMaggio as a kid. The point is, you just never know what might spark a lively connection in a situation like this. So, rule number one, assume that your guests will look for common ground.

In fact, if your idea of a guest list is one where everyone is the same age, with the same occupation, all with generally the same background, you could end up with a pretty dull affair. Don't go out of your way to invite half red-state conservatives and half blue-state liberals, but look for a mix of people who see life a little differently. They'll all like the novelty.

Next, mix up the seating so that each group has maximum exposure to the other. In other words, don't let people seat themselves, and don't plant the

old friends at one end of the table and the new friends at the other. Old friends, left to their own devices, will gravitate toward each other like a flock of crows. Separate husbands and wives, for sure, or golfing buddies, or you and the girlfriend you talk to six times a day. Having said that, I prefer boy-girl-boy-girl, but that's just me.

There is an art to seating people at a dinner

WHEN THINGS GO TERRIBLY WRONG

I did a mini-survey of friends and acquaintances to gather some stories about the worst dinner party they've ever attended or, God forbid, hosted. Has this happened to you? My son, Anthony, Jr., thinks my next book should be called *World's Worst Dinner Parties Ever*, or *That's Not Masonite—That's Veal*. Well, here's Chapter One. CS

MARY De ANGELIS (my mom): Never invite a vegetarian or what they now call a "vegan." Sure, there's always plenty of veggies for them to "graze" on, but they tend to glower at the other "carnivores" nibbling on their spareribs. My cousin is one of those and every time she's invited somewhere, how she *eats* is the whole conversation. And if, Madonn', someone should say, "Boy, I love ribs," get ready for a twenty-minute tirade about the force-feeding of baby calves, how cattle are slaughtered, what they do with the innards, etc. She often brings photos. Sometimes people bolt from the table with their hands over their mouths.

JEAN CUSAMANO: The worst party I ever hosted began with a simple idea: invite two couples who didn't know each other but happened to live on the same block in North Caldwell. Only after the meal began did they realize that one was suing

the other guy's neighbor (and dear friend) over mansionizing his new house. My husband, though he's a doctor, knows all about local zoning laws, so he jumps right in. The argument got so nasty that the plaintiff got his lawyer on the speakerphone to tell the other guy he was an idiot. When the last couple left, there was a key scratch along the side of their brand-new Lexus. The guy was yelling to Bruce, "I'm going to sue *you*, you bastard," as he drove away. Some party.

MUSIC ♪

party that I don't profess to have mastered. I have often, with the best intentions, put Mr. Opinionated #1 right across from Mr. Opinionated #2, and boy, did the sparks fly. Some people can spend hours figuring these things out. I just say, go with your instincts. Look for common interests and matching personalities, like a good cook next to a big eater. Or sometimes opposites make the best dinner companions—a shy person next to a gregarious one, a lawyer next to an art lover, a young mother-to-be with an old-timer. And tell your husband that it's *his* job as well as yours to make everyone feel included. Pump him full of pre-party information about the new people so he can engage them beyond, "So, how're ya doin'?"

Once you've decided on the right mix of people, send out mailed invitations, usually three weeks ahead of time. Why mailed invitations and not just a phone call? It's a nice touch, plus your guests can pin it on their bulletin board as a reminder. Because it's only five invitations (for five couples), you can

GINNY SACRIMONI: You invite a reformed gambler, a reformed drug addict, a reformed wife beater, or a reformed anything over and you're asking for one head-throbbing evening. "Blah, blah, hated life, blah, blah, saw the face of God, blah, blah, I'm special, blah, blah, blah." They'll look right at you, or at me, at least, and say, "You know, there's an Eaters Anonymous, too," like it was any of their damn business, you know what I mean? Johnny threw a guy out of the house one night who saw me grab a biscotti and said, "Ginny, you don't really need that." The nerve!

GABRIELLA DANTE: Worst dinner party ever? Silvio has this cute cousin from Fairfield who's really into breast feeding. Twelve people sitting around a table eating osso buco and she pulls a breast out of her halter top and sticks it in little Bobo's mouth. My dad almost choked. A friend of our daughter Heather snuck down the stairs and took a picture with his cell phone. Then Rocco, the lush, tries to place an order for low fat. Sure, it's natural, but not at my table, thank you very much.

JANICE SOPRANO BACCILIERI: Rule of thumb: never invite a widow or divorcee for at least three months after the fact. I know—you'll be victimized by what I call morbid clinging. A sudden hysterical crying jag brought on by "Joey's favorite pasta" can ruin any dinner. Pretty soon people will be saying what a great guy Joey was, if he died, and what a loser, if he ran off with the babysitter, and it only makes things worse. All of sudden you're not having dinner, you're having grief therapy! Everybody goes home thinking life is a bunch of crap, which, of course, is only half-right.

handwrite them on nice stock or even do a little watercolor painting on each. Think of something more striking than a machine-made card that says "Come on by!"

At a dinner party for twelve, the dining table is the focal point of the event. See it as a one-time design project that fits the mood you hope to create. Here are some simple touches that can make your table inviting and charming.

• Layer tablecloths for a lush effect. You can layer white on white, or embroidered white on plain cotton, or you can mix colors, with a base tablecloth in red or navy and an overlay in a sheer metallic silver or gold. If the table itself is beautiful, opt for a colorful runner rather than a cloth.

• Use candles. Place plain votive candles on a trio of rectangular mirrors or float candles in long shallow acrylic boxes filled with water. You can find these boxes online or perhaps at a local candle shop.

• To get away from a big center floral arrangement, which often blocks conversation and has to be moved anyway, cluster tiny glass vases near each place setting. To find the right kind of miniature flowers for this, ask a florist.

• Create place cards and even menu cards, if you're so inspired. You can do something as simple as split a wine cork and place a simple name card in the split. Or you can attach a name card with a ribbon to a small bottle of high-end olive oil as a gift, or to a small bag of after-dinner truffles. If you want to print out the menu, get the computer wiz in the family to print them out using a nice font and card stock.

When you choose a menu for twelve, keep in mind that there are four distinct ways to present it. (It's great to have cooking school grads as friends.) One, *restaurant-style:* the guests sit and you bring them one plate at a time, with no serving dishes on the table. This might take extra help in the kitchen. Two, what is called "*French-style*": the food is on a platter, or a series of them, and presented to each guest individually so they can serve themselves. The platters remain on the table for second helpings. This demands a waiter, even if it's you. Three, *family-style,* the one most of us tend to use: plattered food is placed on the table and guests help themselves. Fourth is *buffet,* discussed in

WINE SUGGESTIONS

Aspirino di Aversa
{ a white wine from the Naples area }

Montepulciano d'Abruzzo
{ a red wine from the Abruzzo region }

Salice Salentino
{ a red wine from the Puglia region }

Chapter 1. At a nice affair like this, you might need to rent food warmers or a chafing dish so that the food doesn't get cold between servings.

The table, the setting, the food, the wine selection, all enhance the mood for this kind of party, but the real focal point is the guests. Are they enjoying themselves? Are they enjoying each other? Mixing old and new friends is inherently risky, but the chances are things will work out fine. And if they don't? What have you lost? One evening in your life. What have you gained? Valuable experience about what and what not to do—or whom not to sit next to whom—for the future. And you'll probably have an amusing story to tell at your next dinner for twelve.

prosecco

Prosecco is a sparkling white wine made primarily near the town of Conegliano, in Italy's Veneto district, but enjoyed by Italians of all regions. Unlike champagne, fermented in bottles for years, Prosecco is aged in pressurized tanks and goes from vine to table in under two years. It is light and dry with a fruity aroma and a lower alcohol level than most wines. Wine snobs think it is a little boring, but real people love it. Serve it as an apertif, with appetizers, or perhaps with a dessert. *Buon appetito!*

MELON AND PROSCIUTTO

Serves 12

INGREDIENTS

2 large cantaloupes or small honeydew melons, chilled

36 paper-thin slices imported Italian prosciutto, such as prosciutto di Parma (about 12 ounces)

Freshly ground black pepper

Lime or lemon wedges for garnish

PREPARATION

Cut each melon into 12 slices. Scoop out and discard the seeds and cut off the skin. Place 2 slices on each serving plate.

Drape the prosciutto over the melon slices. Sprinkle with pepper. Garnish with lime or lemon wedges.

BAKED ZITI "IN BIANCO"

Serves 8 to 12

INGREDIENTS

Béchamel Sauce (page 101)

1 pound ziti

Salt

4 tablespoons (½ stick) unsalted butter

6 ounces fresh mozzarella, cut into ½-inch cubes

6 ounces smoked mozzarella, cut into ½-inch cubes

4 ounces thick-sliced boiled ham, cut into narrow strips

½ cup freshly grated Parmigiano-Reggiano

PREPARATION

Bring at least 4 quarts of salted water to a boil in a large pot. Add the ziti. Cook, stirring frequently, until the ziti is al dente, tender yet still firm to the bite.

Meanwhile, preheat the oven to 350°F. Butter an 11½ x 8½ x 2-inch baking dish.

Drain the ziti. In a large bowl, toss the ziti with the butter. Spoon a thin layer of sauce into the baking dish. Make a layer of about one-quarter of the pasta. Sprinkle with one-third of the fresh and smoked mozzarella and ham and 2 tablespoons of the grated cheese. Make a second thin layer of sauce. Repeat layering the pasta, mozzarella, ham, and sauce, ending with sauce and grated cheese.

Bake the pasta for 40 minutes, or until the sauce is bubbling and the top is lightly browned. Let stand 10 minutes before serving.

BÉCHAMEL SAUCE

Makes 4 cups

INGREDIENTS

4 cups milk
4 tablespoons (½ stick) unsalted butter
¼ cup all-purpose flour
Pinch of freshly grated nutmeg
Salt and freshly ground white pepper

PREPARATION

Heat the milk in a medium saucepan until small bubbles form around the edges.

Meanwhile, melt the butter in a large saucepan over medium-low heat. Add the flour and stir well. Cook, stirring, 2 minutes.

Very slowly begin adding the hot milk in a thin stream, whisking constantly. The sauce will look lumpy at first, but it will smooth out as you continue to add the milk. When all of the milk has been added, stir in the nutmeg and salt and pepper to taste. Raise the heat to medium and bring the sauce to a simmer. Cook 2 minutes more. Remove from the heat and pour into a bowl.

Use immediately, or place a piece of plastic wrap directly on the surface to prevent a skin from forming and chill. (The sauce can be made up to 24 hours before using.)

VEAL ROLLATINI WITH PEAS

Serves 12

INGREDIENTS

1 pound lean ground pork

1 small garlic clove, finely chopped

2 teaspoons finely chopped fresh rosemary

½ teaspoon salt, plus more to taste

Freshly ground black pepper

24 thin slices veal scallopini, about 3 x 4 x ¼ inch thick

2 tablespoons olive oil

1 cup dry white wine

One 28-ounce can Italian peeled tomatoes, chopped

One 10-ounce package frozen baby peas, partially thawed

Chopped fresh flat-leaf parsley for garnish

PREPARATION

In a large bowl, combine the pork, garlic, rosemary, salt, and pepper to taste. Form the mixture into 24 small sausage shapes about 3 inches long.

Sprinkle the veal slices with salt and pepper. Place one sausage at the short end of a piece of veal. Roll up the veal to enclose the sausage. With a toothpick, pin the roll closed in the center, parallel to the roll, or tie it closed with string. Repeat with the remaining veal and filling.

In a large skillet, heat the olive oil over medium heat. Add as many of the rolls as will fit comfortably without crowding. Brown the rolls on all sides, about 10 minutes. Transfer the rolls to a plate. Brown the remaining rolls in the same way.

Pour the wine into the skillet and cook 1 minute, scraping the bottom of the pan. Add the tomatoes and salt to taste. Return the rolls to the skillet, reduce the heat to low, and partially cover the pan. Cook, turning the rolls occasionally, for 20 minutes, or until the rolls are tender when pierced with a fork. If there is too much liquid when the rolls are done, remove them to a plate and simmer the sauce until thickened. (The rollatini can be made up to 24 hours ahead to this point. Let cool, then cover and refrigerate. Reheat the rolls over low heat before serving, adding a little water to the pan if needed.)

Add the peas to the skillet and simmer 5 minutes more. Transfer the rolls to a platter. Remove the toothpicks or strings and spoon the sauce over the top. Garnish with chopped parsley.

BAKED PEPPERS AU GRATIN

Serves 12

INGREDIENTS

8 large bell peppers, preferably a mix of green, yellow, red, and orange

½ cup plain dry bread crumbs, preferably homemade from Italian bread

¼ cup finely chopped fresh flat-leaf parsley

⅓ cup olive oil

1 teaspoon salt

Freshly ground pepper to taste

PREPARATION

Preheat the oven to 400°F. Oil one or two roasting pans large enough to hold the sliced peppers in a single layer.

Cut the peppers lengthwise in half and remove the seeds, cores, and white membranes. Cut each half into ½ inch-wide strips. Put the peppers in the pan(s). Add the remaining ingredients and toss well.

Bake 40 to 50 minutes, or until the peppers are tender and browned. Serve hot or at room temperature.

PANNA COTTA WITH RASPBERRY SAUCE AND BLUEBERRIES

Serves 12

INGREDIENTS

Three ¼-ounce envelopes unflavored gelatin

½ cup cold water

1 quart half-and-half

2 cups heavy cream

1 vanilla bean or 2 teaspoons pure vanilla extract

One 3-inch strip lemon zest

⅓ cup sugar

RASPBERRY SAUCE

Two 10-ounce packages frozen raspberries in syrup, thawed

2 tablespoons sugar, or more to taste

1 teaspoon fresh lemon juice

1 teaspoon cornstarch, mixed with 2 tablespoons water

1 cup blueberries for garnish

PREPARATION

In a small bowl, sprinkle the gelatin over the cold water. Set aside to soften.

Combine the half-and-half, cream, vanilla bean (if using vanilla extract, reserve it until later), lemon zest, and sugar in a medium saucepan and bring to a simmer over medium-high heat. Remove from the heat and add the softened gelatin. Stir until the gelatin is completely dissolved.

Discard the lemon zest. If you used the vanilla bean, remove it, slit the bean lengthwise with a small sharp knife, and scrape the seeds out. Stir the seeds into the cream mixture. (Or add the vanilla extract.)

Divide the cream mixture among twelve 6-ounce ramekins or custard cups. Cover and refrigerate until the panna cotta is set, at least 4 hours, or overnight.

To make the raspberry sauce, puree the berries with their syrup, the sugar, and lemon juice in a food processor or blender. Strain the mixture through a fine sieve into a small saucepan.

Bring the puree to a simmer over medium heat. Add the cornstarch mixture and cook, stirring frequently, until slightly thickened, about 2 minutes. Remove from the heat and let cool, then pour into a tightly sealed container and refrigerate. (The sauce can be stored in the refrigerator up to 3 days.)

To serve, dip the bottom of one ramekin into a bowl of hot water for 10 seconds. Run a thin knife around the edge of the cream. Invert the cream onto a serving plate. Repeat with the remaining ramekins.

Spoon some of the sauce around the creams. Scatter a few blueberries on top. Serve immediately.

Chapter 6

HOLIDAYS

W hy do we dread holidays? Why does the very thought of Thanksgiving or Christmas send many of us scurrying to the wine bar or otherwise feeling sorry for ourselves for all the work we think we have to do? This creates a very bad frame of mind. We become more interested in just getting through these big holidays than savoring them. In Italy, many holiday gatherings, like the annual St. Joseph's Day, are feast days: joyous, loving, gut-busting celebrations. Over here we seem to be losing that sense of innocent family festivity. Well, let's try to get it back.

I've included some simple Italian menus below for holiday meals like Christmas Day, Easter, and the aforementioned St. Joseph's Day, a Catholic holiday on March 19th of each year that honors all fathers, especially the father of Christ, Joseph. And I've included some decorating ideas for Easter. But our main focus here is on Christmas Eve. It's a big event in many Italian-American households for reasons that will soon become clear. It's the big meal, the big gathering, and the big family trek to midnight Mass, assuming anyone can still move after the meal.

Whether for Christmas Day or Christmas Eve, decorating the house is job one. My view, probably apparent by now, is to keep the decorations clean, simple, and imaginative. In the same way you might create a color scheme for a confirmation party, create one for Christmas. I'll pick three traditional colors: red, white, and gold. Hang a white feather wreath or a wreath crafted from winter-white tallow berries on the front door. For a Christmas Day or Christmas Eve dinner, decorate the table like one big Christmas present. Start with a floor-length white tablecloth, lay two floor-length red or gold satin runners across each other like ribbons around a package, and place a big wire-supported bow in the middle. Take plain inexpensive gold ornament balls and write each guest's name on one as place cards.

Repeat and amplify the color scheme around the house. Trim your tree with white fairy lights and ball ornaments in white and gold. Wind gossamer metallic gold ribbon between the branches. Fill up vases with red and white flowers, maybe roses, and

look for other situations where a touch of red, white, or gold might illuminate the room.

This is just one idea, of course. We've all had enough experience with Christmas to know what colors, what kind of decorative items, and what seasonal accessories, from candle-powered chimes to a handmade Nativity scene, fit our own style. What I am suggesting here is that, like a good interior designer, you work on a blend of colors, shapes, and objects that play off of each other, create a distinct mood, and don't give the impression that you just took some stuff from the attic marked "Christmas Décor" and threw it up like you were dragging yourself through another Christmas season. Do you wear the same dress every Christmas Day? Of course not. Nor should you dress your house the same. Try something new. Spray paint some mid-sized terracotta pots gold and fill them with a flood of white flowers. Or create one big bowl brimming with red-

WHEN CHRISTMAS WAS CHRISTMAS

To get a sense of what Christmas was like back in the days when all those immigrant-filled Little Italys peppered the American landscape, I sat down with someone who would know, Tony's aging Uncle Junior. Here are his memories.

Uncle Junior: Your son gave me a $10 gift card to the video store this year. What's that about?
Carmela: No, Uncle Junior, I wanted to talk about when you were a little boy growing up in the First Ward in Newark. What was Christmas like then?
Junior: Oh, then. Then it was better than now, I'll tell you that. I got hand-me-downs from a cousin I hated and Ercoli got my clothes and Johnny got his, so present-wise, it wasn't much, but who cared? There was no Giorgio Versace back then.
Carmela: But the food was good, right?
Junior: Oh, yeah, and I got a nickel once.
Carmela: The food. . .

Junior: *Capitone.* Oh, how I loved the *capitone.* Your grandmother, see. . .
Carmela: Not my grandmother. Tony's grandmother.
Junior: Whatever. She'd buy these live eels and stick them in the bathtub until Christmas Eve, just let them wiggle around in there, no one took a bath for a week, then she'd fix 'em up nice, cut off their heads—whack!—and pull their skin off with a pair of pliers.
Carmela: Sounds delightful.
Junior: And the *caposelle.* You take a sheep's head, see, and you roast it and then serve it with the brains, the eyeballs, the sinus cavities, the whole thing. It was delicious. I wonder why they don't eat that anymore?
Carmela: Good question. That's it . . . live eels and a sheep's skull?
Junior: Don't forget the *pesce stocco,* the stockfish, which stunk up the whole neighborhood; the hot chestnuts, I liked those; the fruit with fennel, which helps your digestion, you know. That's about it. Uncle Vin would start singing old songs, but my dad always told him to shut up.
Carmela: Do you miss those days, Uncle Junior?
Junior: What is a gift card, anyway? Why didn't he just give me cash?
Carmela: Thank you, Uncle Jun.
Junior: For what? What did I do?

and-white-colored peppermint bark, slabs of white and milk chocolate with bits of peppermint candy. There's a lot you can do with three simple colors—or twelve, if that's your taste.

A couple of more ideas: Create a table centerpiece using fresh-cut greens arranged in pedestal bowls or gold urns. Place two or three votive candles in front of each place setting, and contrast white plates with gold charger plates underneath. Find a large glass cylinder vase and fill it with gold metallic balls in various sizes, then arrange a set of fairy lights around the cylinder on the mantel to reflect the gold balls. Or just fill the cylinder full of white fairy lights, perhaps battery powered, if you can find them. It's striking—a vase full of light.

Once you've adorned the house and table, think about a meal that might be a departure from the traditional holiday menu, like turkey, stuffing, and pumpkin pie. For Italian-Americans, the grand Christmas Eve tradition is called "The Feast of the Seven Fishes." As a way of getting away from the Christmas we've all come to fear and dislike—long shopping lines, agonizing over the right expensive present, all the commercial hype and pressures—I thought I'd focus on this one family feast as something you might want to try. And thanks to a very

QUICK EASTER DECORATING IDEAS

Think light, fresh, springy. Clear glass plates or white plates and cloth napkins in light green, light pink, light yellow. Use pastel-dyed eggs as place cards. Write each name on a shell, and place in a clear glass egg cup or a little crafted bird's nest.

Place spring flowers everywhere. Purple crocuses in terra-cotta pots. Clear vases of pink and mauve tulips. Flats of wheatgrass planted in rustic wooden boxes, like miniature lawns. Trim a buffet table in fresh daisies—snip off the entire stem, then use double-sided tape to attach the flower heads along the edges of the table.

Set off menu items—especially the Easter Dessert Pie and the Easter Sweet Bread—by creating a stand-alone dessert table. Drape a card table with a floor-length white tablecloth. Create an Easter Egg Tree in the center: anchor a tree branch in a plant holder with small stones, then decorate the tree with pastel satin ribbons, dyed eggs, miniature Easter baskets filled with jelly beans, even little chocolate bunnies.

knowledgeable woman in the field of Italian-American culture, Natalie del Greco of the Newark Public Library, I learned a lot about the origins of this ritual. Here's how Natalie describes The Feast of the Seven Fishes:

"From my research, here's what we know. We think that The Feast of the Seven Fishes originated in Sicily, but that's just an educated guess. The significance of the number seven is also a bit of a mystery. It could symbolize, variously, the seven sacraments of the Catholic Church; the Seven Deadly Sins of man, i.e., pride, envy, gluttony, lust, anger, greed, and sloth, to refresh your memory; the seven days it took Mary and Joseph to travel to Bethlehem for the birth of the Christ Child; or the fact that seven of the Apostles were fishermen. Of course, if you think the feast may have originated a

FISH AND FOOD POISONING
by Artie Bucco

As a restaurateur, I deal with fish daily and I know a good, fresh, tasteful piece of fish from a going-bad, going-tasteless, and maybe going-poisonous one. Please, allow me to give you a few fish buying and eating tips, first for gilled fish, then for shellfish.

Fish with Gills

- Smell it. If it stinks, enough said. If the whole fish market stinks, move on. They don't say something "smells fishy" for nothing.

- Look at the eyes. Bright, clear, protruding eyes are good. Cloudy, pink, sunken eyes are not so good. Some fish, like grouper, have cloudier eyes than others and are still fresh. But bright eyes is generally the rule.

- Look at the gills. They should be bright red or pink. That means the fish has been breathing recently. If the gills are gray, brown, or green, or covered with mucus, well, you figure it out.

- Press the flesh. If it bounces back, you're in good shape. If the fish is whole, look to see that the skin is shiny, with scales that adhere tightly. If it is in steak or fillet form, the flesh should be firm, with no browning on the edges and no bruising or reddening of the flesh from retention of blood. If it's in a package, make sure there's a minimum of liquid; seafood stored in liquid deteriorates fast.

Shellfish

- Shellfish scare a lot of people, and for good reason. A bad mussel or scallop can make you sick as a dog. Shellfish may be sold live, cooked, or freshly shucked. Each should be investigated on its own terms.

- If you're buying live shellfish, the shells of clams, oysters, or mussels should be tightly closed and look moist. Discard any with shells that are opened or cracked. If the fish are preshucked, the meat should be plump and covered with clear or slightly opalescent liquor—in other words, a cloudy juice.

- Scallops are not sold live here because they are highly perishable and are generally shucked at sea immediately. Fresh ones from the fish market should have a firm texture and sweet odor. A sour or iodine smell means they've turned on you.

- Live crabs and lobsters should move around like they're, you know, alive. The tail of a live lobster should curl up tightly, not hang like a wet rag when you pick him up. Sometimes live crabs and lobsters are kept refrigerated, but even then, they should move a little. Cooked crabs and lobsters that you buy in a market should be bright red in color and not smell bad. Picked meat from both should generally be white with red or brown tints.

- Being that it's the most common shellfish people eat, knowing your way around shrimp is very important. Raw shrimp should be firm and have only a mild odor, not a stink. The shells, in general, should be translucent and have no blackened edges or black spots. Cooked shrimp should be firm, not mushy, and have no stink either. The color of cooked shrimp meat should be white with a little red or pink tint. Remember, if it smells bad, throw it away, please. A lot of people just refuse to throw away bad shrimp or fish. They think it's a waste of money. Wrong. It's the presence of a brain.

From the Kitchen of Carmela

Spiked Eggnog (for 12)

Large saucepan: Heat 2 quarts eggnog over low heat almost to boil. Remove from stove, stir in 1 1/4 cups Tia Maria. Pour in punch bowl and garnish with grated nutmeg. Easy, but watch the heavy drinkers.

From the Kitchen of Carmela

Spiked Hot Chocolate (for 4)

Double boiler: Melt 1/2 cup semi-sweet chocolate chips. In small saucepan, heat 3 cups milk, 1 cup half-and-half, 1 cup sugar almost to boil. Add 1 cup of this milk mixture to the melted chips, stir until smooth. Gradually add remaining milk, stir until smooth. Add 1/2 cup rum and 1/2 cup hazelnut liqueur and heat well. Pour into mugs, add a dollop of whipped cream and grated milk chocolate (optional); serve with a candy cane stirrer. (Tony loves!)

From the Kitchen of Carmela

Hot Buttered Rum

Put 3 ounces dark rum, a lemon peel twist, 1 stick cinnamon, and 2 cloves in a large mug. Heat 1/3 cup apple cider almost to boil and pour in rum mixture. Add a tablespoon of sweet butter and stir until melted. Pour into mug and garnish with grated nutmeg.
A classic!

From the Kitchen of Carmela

Candy Cane Martini (Rosie's recipe)

Dip the rims of martini glasses into a bowl of fresh lime juice, then into a dish of finely-crushed candy canes. Mix 5 parts vodka (the good kind) to 1 part peppermint schnapps in an ice-filled cocktail shaker. Shake and pour into the rimmed glasses.

little north of Sicily, you might conclude that it stands for the Seven Hills of Rome.

"We do know that seven fish dishes are traditionally served because the meal signifies the Catholic tradition of abstaining from meat. The church dictates that there are specific days of the year that are called Days of Abstinence—formerly every Friday, but more recently, Ash Wednesday, Good Friday, and all the Fridays of Lent. As every schoolchild knows, on those Fridays you eat fish, not beef, pork, or lamb. Why Southern Italians decided to make Christmas Eve into a Day of Abstinence, or a *vigilia di magro,* is another head-scratcher. Perhaps they wanted to use the occasion of the sacrifice of not eating meat—a big sacrifice for some—to focus on the sacrifice of Christ.

"Nowadays, seven fish dishes in one meal are too much for some, so they cheat a little and reduce the number to three or five. The important thing is to not eat meat, which, to many diet-conscious Americans, is not that big a deal, but you get the point. Among Italian-American immigrants from the 1870s through the 1920s, a multi-fish meal was traditionally a luxury and a once-a-year holiday indulgence. Fresh fish was expensive and not often consumed in such large quantities.

"Common sense tells us that any time we consciously *don't* eat something we enjoy, we are re-directing our attention and even our lives, at least momentarily. Hopefully not eating meat on Christmas Eve continues to redirect our attention back to family, friends, and the original meaning of Christmas."

Thank you, Natalie. There is nothing I can add to that beautiful sentiment except to say Merry Christmas to all, no matter how, where, and with whom you choose to spend the holiday season.

Christmas Eve
SPAGHETTI WITH RED CLAM SAUCE

Serves 4 to 6

INGREDIENTS

3 pounds very small clams, such as Manila or mahogany clams, or
   New Zealand cockles (or mussels)

4 garlic cloves, thinly sliced

Pinch of crushed red pepper

⅓ cup olive oil

2 tablespoons chopped fresh flat-leaf parsley

2 pints grape or cherry tomatoes, cut in half

Pinch of salt

1 pound spaghetti or linguine

PREPARATION

Scrub the clams (or mussels) with a brush under cold running water and debeard.
Place them in a bowl and rinse well; rinse several times, until there is no sand left
in the bottom of the bowl. Discard any clams that have broken shells or that do
not close up tightly.

In a skillet large enough to hold all of the clams and the cooked pasta, cook the
garlic and red pepper in the oil over medium heat until the garlic is golden, about
3 minutes. Stir in the parsley, then add the tomatoes and salt. Cook until the
tomatoes are softened, about 5 minutes.

Add the clams, cover the pot, and cook 5 minutes, or until all of the clams are
opened. Discard any clams that do not open.

Meanwhile, in a large pot, bring at least 4 quarts of salted water to a boil. Add the pasta
and cook, stirring frequently, until the pasta is al dente, tender yet firm to the bite.

Scoop out a little of the pasta cooking water and set it aside. Drain the pasta and
toss it into the pan with the clams. Stir well, adding a little of the pasta cooking
water if the mixture seems dry.

Serve immediately.

LINGUINE WITH SPICY SHRIMP AND TOMATO SAUCE

Serves 4 to 6

INGREDIENTS

1½ pounds large shrimp, shelled and deveined

3 large garlic cloves, finely chopped

Pinch of crushed red pepper

¼ cup olive oil

2 tablespoons chopped fresh flat-leaf parsley

One 28-ounce can Italian peeled tomatoes, drained and chopped

Pinch of salt

1 pound linguine or spaghetti

PREPARATION

Rinse the shrimp and pat dry. Cut the shrimp into ½-inch pieces.

In a skillet large enough to hold all of the ingredients, including the cooked pasta, cook the garlic and crushed red pepper in the olive oil over medium heat until the garlic is golden, about 3 minutes. Stir in the parsley, then add the tomatoes and salt. Bring the sauce to a simmer. Cook, stirring occasionally, until the tomatoes are soft and the sauce has thickened, about 20 minutes. (The sauce can be prepared ahead to this point. Reheat before finishing the dish.)

Stir the shrimp into the simmering sauce. Cook 1 minute, or until the shrimp are cooked through.

Meanwhile, in a large pot, bring at least 4 quarts salted water to boiling. Add the spaghetti and cook, stirring frequently, until al dente, tender yet firm to the bite.

Scoop out a little of the pasta cooking water and set it aside. Drain the pasta and toss it into the pan with the shrimp sauce. Stir well, adding a little of the pasta water if the mixture seems dry.

Serve immediately.

BACCALÀ FRITTA

Fried Salt Cod

Serves 6

INGREDIENTS

1½ pounds boneless, skinless baccalà, cut into serving pieces

4 large eggs

1 cup all-purpose flour

½ teaspoon salt

Freshly ground pepper

Olive oil for frying

Lemon wedges

Sprigs of fresh parsley for garnish

PREPARATION

Place the baccalà in a large bowl of cold water and refrigerate, changing the water at least 3 times a day, for 1 to 2 days, or until the water no longer tastes salty. Drain the baccalà and dry it well with paper towels. You can keep the baccalà in the refrigerator for at least 1 day after it is ready. (Or substitute fresh cod fillets; they do not need to be soaked.)

In a shallow bowl, whisk the eggs, 3 tablespoons of the flour, the salt, and pepper to taste until blended. Spread the remaining 1 cup flour on a piece of wax paper.

Pour about ½ inch of olive oil into a large skillet. Heat the oil over medium heat until a bit of the egg mixture sizzles when dropped in the pan. Roll one piece of fish in the flour and shake off the excess. Dip it in the egg mixture, coating it on all sides. Carefully slip the fish into the hot oil. Coat some or all of the remaining pieces in the same way, adding only enough pieces to the pan as will fit comfortably without crowding. Fry the fish until a deep golden brown on the first side, about 4 minutes. Turn the pieces over and brown on the other side, about 3 minutes more. Drain the fish on paper towels. (Fry any remaining fish.)

Serve hot with lemon wedges, garnished with parsley sprigs.

OCTOPUS SALAD

Serves 6

INGREDIENTS

1 octopus (about 3½ pounds), thawed if frozen and cleaned
2 garlic cloves, lightly crushed
1 bay leaf
Salt

SALAD

¼ cup extra virgin olive oil
2 tablespoons red wine vinegar
Pinch of crushed red pepper
Salt
2 celery ribs, sliced (include some of the green leaves)
¼ cup coarsely chopped fresh flat-leaf parsley
Lettuce leaves for serving

PREPARATION

Bring a large pot of water to a boil. Add the octopus, garlic, bay leaf, and salt to taste. Partially cover the pot and cook the octopus until tender when pierced with a fork, about 1 to 1¼ hours. Drain the octopus.

In a large bowl, whisk together the oil, vinegar, red pepper, and salt to taste. Cut the octopus into bite-sized pieces and add them to the bowl, stirring well. (Some people use just the tentacles.) Add the celery and parsley and stir.

Serve warm or lightly chilled on a bed of lettuce leaves.

SHRIMP ARAGONATE

Baked Stuffed Shrimp

Serves 6

INGREDIENTS

1 cup fresh bread crumbs made from Italian or French bread (with the
   crusts removed)

⅓ cup chopped fresh flat-leaf parsley

1 large garlic clove, finely chopped

Salt and freshly ground pepper

About ¼ cup olive oil

1½ pounds large shrimp, shelled and deveined

2 large lemons, cut into wedges

PREPARATION

Preheat the oven to 450°F. Oil a large baking pan.

In a medium bowl, combine the bread crumbs, parsley, garlic, and salt and pepper
to taste. Stir in ¼ cup oil, or just enough to moisten the crumbs.

Arrange the shrimp in the pan in a single layer, curling each shrimp into a circle.
Spoon a little of the bread crumb mixture onto each shrimp.

Bake until the crumbs are browned and the shrimp are cooked through when cut
in the thickest part, about 10 minutes.

Serve hot or at room temperature, with the lemon wedges.

PIZZA DI SCAROLA

'Shcarole Pie ⊛ Escarole Pie

Serves 8

INGREDIENTS

1 package (2½ teaspoons) active
   dry yeast

1⅓ cups warm water (100° to 110°F)

About 4 cups all-purpose flour

1½ teaspoons salt

2 tablespoons olive oil

FILLING

2 large bunches escarole (about 2½ pounds),
   washed well and trimmed

Salt

4 large garlic cloves, finely chopped

Pinch of crushed red pepper

⅓ cup olive oil

One 2-ounce can anchovy fillets, drained and chopped

3 tablespoons capers, drained and chopped

½ cup sliced imported black olives

PREPARATION

In a small bowl, sprinkle the yeast over the warm water. Let stand 5 minutes, or until the yeast is softened. Stir until dissolved.

In a large mixer bowl or in a food processor, combine the flour and salt. Add the yeast mixture and oil and mix or process until a soft dough forms and pulls away from the sides of the bowl. Add a little more flour if the dough is too wet. It should be smooth and feel moist but not sticky. Scrape the dough onto a board and knead for 1 minute. Shape the dough into a ball.

Oil a large bowl. Add the dough, turning it once to grease the top. Cover and let rise in a warm place until doubled in volume, about 1½ hours.

To make the filling, place the escarole in a large pot with 1 cup water. Add a little salt (remember that the other ingredients are salty, so add just a little). Cook over medium heat, stirring occasionally, until the escarole is tender, about 10 minutes. Drain and let cool.

Wrap the escarole in a towel and squeeze out the liquid. Chop the escarole into ½-inch pieces.

In a large skillet, cook the garlic and red pepper in the oil over medium heat until the garlic is golden, about 3 minutes. Add the anchovies and stir until they are dissolved. Stir in the capers. Add the escarole and olives and stir until well mixed. Cook 10 minutes, stirring occasionally. Taste for seasoning. Remove from the heat and let cool.

Preheat the oven to 425°F. Oil a 12-inch pizza pan.

Divide the ball of dough in half. Roll out one piece of the dough on a lightly floured surface to a 12-inch circle. Center the dough in the pizza pan. Spread the filling over the dough, leaving a 1-inch border around the edges.

Roll out the remaining dough to a 12-inch circle and place it on top of the filling. Press the edges of the dough together firmly to seal. With a small sharp knife, make several slits in the top of the dough to allow the steam to escape.

Bake the pie 40 minutes, or until browned and crisp. Serve immediately, or transfer the pizza to a rack and let cool to room temperature.

SEA BASS WITH TOMATOES, OLIVES, AND CAPERS

Serves 4

INGREDIENTS

1 small onion, finely chopped

¼ cup olive oil

2 garlic cloves, finely chopped

2 tablespoons chopped fresh flat-leaf parsley

2 cups canned tomatoes, chopped, with their juice

2 tablespoons capers, rinsed and drained

Salt and freshly ground pepper

½ cup pitted black oil-cured olives, roughly chopped

1½ pounds Chilean sea bass or cod fillets

PREPARATION

In a large skillet, cook the onion in the oil over medium heat until tender, about 8 minutes. Stir in the garlic and parsley and cook 2 minutes more.

Add the tomatoes, capers, a pinch of salt, and pepper to taste. Bring to a simmer and cook 15 minutes, or until the sauce is thickened. Stir in the olives. Place the fish in the pan and baste it with the sauce. Cover and simmer 5 minutes, or until the fish is cooked through.

Serve hot.

ZUPPA INGLESE

Neapolitan Trifle

Serves 10 to 12

INGREDIENTS

CUSTARD

3 cups milk

1 cup heavy cream

½ cup sugar

6 large egg yolks

½ cup all-purpose flour

2 teaspoons pure vanilla extract

One 12-ounce all-butter pound cake,
   cut into thin slices

½ cup Marsala, cherry liqueur, or rum

⅔ cup sour cherry preserves

WHIPPED CREAM

1 cup very cold heavy cream

2 teaspoons confectioners' sugar

1 teaspoon vanilla extract

Fresh berries or shaved chocolate for garnish

PREPARATION

In a large heavy saucepan, bring 2 cups of the milk, the cream, and sugar to a simmer over medium heat, stirring to dissolve the sugar. Remove from the heat.

In a large heatproof bowl, whisk the egg yolks and the remaining 1 cup milk until blended. Place the flour in a fine-mesh strainer, shake it over the egg yolks, and whisk until smooth. Beat in the hot liquid a little at a time.

When all of the milk has been added, pour the mixture into the saucepan and return it to the heat. Cook over medium heat, stirring constantly with a wooden spoon, until the mixture begins to boil. Reduce the heat and cook 30 seconds more. Remove the pan from the heat and stir in the vanilla. Use the custard immediately or transfer to

a bowl. Cover with plastic wrap, pressing the plastic against the surface of the cream and refrigerate. (The custard can be refrigerated up to 24 hours.)

Place a mixing bowl and beaters in the refrigerator to chill.

In a large serving bowl, make a layer of about one-third of the cake slices. Sprinkle the slices with some of the Marsala. Spread with half of the preserves. Pour on half of the custard. Repeat with a second layer of cake, Marsala, preserves, and custard. Top with the remaining cake slices.

In the chilled bowl, with the chilled beaters, whip the cream with the sugar and vanilla until soft peaks form. Spread the cream on top of the cake. Cover and refrigerate several hours, or overnight.

Just before serving, garnish with fresh berries or shaved chocolate.

MOSTACIOLLI

Spiced Chocolate Cookies

Makes about 6 dozen

INGREDIENTS

2 large eggs

10 tablespoons (1¼ sticks) unsalted
   butter, melted and cooled

½ cup milk

2 teaspoons pure vanilla extract

3 cups unbleached all-purpose flour

1 cup sugar

1 cup finely chopped toasted walnuts

½ cup unsweetened cocoa powder,
   sifted

2½ teaspoons baking powder

1 teaspoon ground cinnamon

1 teaspoon salt

1 teaspoon finely ground pepper

½ teaspoon ground cloves

½ teaspoon freshly grated nutmeg

FROSTING

2 cups confectioners' sugar

2 tablespoons dark rum

About 2 tablespoons milk

PREPARATION

Preheat the oven to 375°F. Line two large baking sheets with foil.

In a medium bowl, whisk the eggs until blended. Add the butter, milk, and vanilla.

In a large mixer bowl, stir together the dry ingredients. Add the butter mixture and stir until blended.

Pinch off small pieces of dough and roll them between the palms of your hands into l-inch balls. Place the balls 1 inch apart on the baking sheets.

Bake 18 to 20 minutes, or until the cookies are puffed and slightly cracked. Cool on the baking sheets on racks.

To make the frosting, in a small bowl, combine the confectioners' sugar, rum, and just enough milk so the mixture is the consistency of heavy cream, stirring until smooth. Dip the top of each cookie in the frosting. Place frosted side up on a rack and let stand until the frosting is firm.

Store in a tightly sealed container. The flavor of these cookies improves as they stand.

PIZZELLE

Lace Cookies

Makes 3 to 4 dozen, depending on size

INGREDIENTS

3½ cups all-purpose flour

1 tablespoon baking powder

Pinch of salt

1½ cups sugar

12 tablespoons (1½ sticks) unsalted butter, melted and cooled

1½ teaspoons anise extract or 1 tablespoon pure vanilla extract

2 teaspoons grated lemon zest

6 large eggs

PREPARATION

Sift together the flour, baking powder, and salt onto a piece of wax paper.

In a large bowl, beat together the sugar, butter, extract, and zest. Add the eggs one at a time, beating well after each addition. Stir in the dry ingredients until blended.

Preheat a pizzelle iron. Every pizzelle maker is a little different, so make the cookies following the manufacturer's directions. Place the cookies on racks to cool.

Store the cookies in a holiday cookie tin or other airtight container. These keep for weeks.

St. Joseph's Day
SFINGI

St. Joseph's Day Zeppole

Makes about 12

INGREDIENTS

RICOTTA CREAM FILLING

One 15-ounce container ricotta

¾ cup confectioners' sugar

1 teaspoon pure vanilla extract

¼ cup mini chocolate chips

1 tablespoon finely chopped candied citron
or orange peel

DOUGH

1 cup water

4 tablespoons (½ stick) unsalted butter

1 teaspoon salt

1 cup all-purpose flour

4 large eggs

Vegetable oil for frying

Candied cherries, cut in half, for garnish

2 tablespoons chopped unsalted pistachios for garnish

Confectioners' sugar

PREPARATION

In a medium bowl, whisk the ricotta, sugar, and vanilla until smooth. Stir in the chocolate chips and candied fruit. Cover and refrigerate several hours, or overnight.

To make the puffs, bring the water, the butter, and salt to a boil over medium heat. Remove from the heat, add the flour all at once, and stir well with a wooden spoon until the flour is completely incorporated.

Return the saucepan to medium heat. Cook, stirring constantly and turning the dough often, until the dough begins to leave a thin film on the bottom of the saucepan, about 3 minutes. (This dries the dough so the puffs will be crisp.) With a rubber spatula, scrape the dough into a large bowl.

Beat in the eggs one at a time. Continue to beat until smooth and shiny, about 2 minutes more.

In a deep heavy saucepan or deep fryer, heat about 3 inches of oil until the temperature reaches 375°F on a deep-frying thermometer, or until a small bit of

the dough dropped into the oil sizzles and turns brown in 1 minute. With a tablespoon, scoop up a rounded spoonful of the batter. And then, with another spoon, carefully push the dough into the oil, so that it does not splash. Continue to add the dough by spoonfuls, without crowding the pan. The dough will puff up and double in size, so do not add too many at one time, or they will stick together. Cook, turning them often, until the dough breaks open, about 4 minutes. Continue to cook 1 to 2 minutes more, or until crisp and golden brown. Remove the fritters with a slotted spoon or skimmer and place them on paper towels to drain. Repeat with the remaining dough. Let cool slightly.

With a small knife, split the fritters partway open. Spoon the cream inside, allowing it to show through the split. Press a cherry half into the cream and sprinkle with pistachios. (If it is not St. Joseph's Day, you can just shake these, without the filling in a bag with cinnamon sugar and serve them like donuts.) Dust the *sfingi* with confectioners' sugar. These are best right after they are made.

Easter
PIZZA RUSTICA
Pizza Gain ❀ Easter Pie

Serves 8 to 10

INGREDIENTS

DOUGH

4 cups all-purpose flour

1½ teaspoons salt

½ cup solid vegetable shortening

8 tablespoons (1 stick) unsalted butter, cut into pieces

2 large eggs, beaten

FILLING

2 pounds ricotta

4 large eggs, lightly beaten

1 cup freshly grated Pecorino Romano

½ teaspoon freshly ground pepper

8 ounces fresh mozzarella, chopped

4 ounces sliced boiled ham, chopped

4 ounces prosciutto, chopped

4 ounces sliced soppressata or other salami, chopped

2 tablespoons chopped fresh flat-leaf parsley

1 egg yolk, beaten with 1 tablespoon water

PREPARATION

Combine the flour and salt in a large mixer bowl or food processor. Add the shortening and butter and stir or pulse until the mixture resembles large crumbs. Add the eggs and stir or pulse briefly until the ingredients come together and form a soft dough. If the dough seems too dry and crumbly, add a little ice water. Don't overmix, or the dough will be tough.

Shape one-third of the dough into a disk. Make a second disk with the remaining dough. Wrap each piece in plastic wrap. Refrigerate 1 hour, or overnight.

To make the filling, in a large bowl, beat the ricotta, eggs, grated cheese, and pepper until well blended. Stir in the chopped cheese, meats, and parsley. (You can substitute other meats or cheese as you prefer, like capicola (*gobagool*), cooked sausage, mild pepperoni, provolone, etc. Some people add sliced hard-cooked eggs too.)

Preheat the oven to 375°F.

On a lightly floured surface, with a floured rolling pin, roll out the large piece of dough to a 15-inch circle. Drape the dough over the rolling pin. Transfer the dough into a 9 x 3-inch springform pan, flattening out any wrinkles against the inside of the pan. Scrape the filling into the pan.

Roll out the remaining dough into a 9½-inch circle. Cut the dough into ¾-inch-wide strips. Place half the strips 1 inch apart over the filling. Turn the pan clockwise and place the remaining strips on top, forming a lattice pattern. Pinch the edges of the strips and bottom layer of dough together to seal. Brush the dough with the beaten egg.

Bake the pie 1 to 1¼ hours, or until the crust is golden and the filling is puffed and set in the center. Cool the pie in the pan on a wire rack for 10 minutes.

Remove the sides of the pan and let the pie cool completely.

Serve at room temperature or lightly chilled. Store in the refrigerator, covered, up to 3 days.

LA PASTIERA

Pizza Gran ❀ Easter Dessert Pie

Serves 8 to 10

INGREDIENTS

FILLING

4 ounces (about ½ cup) hulled wheat (you can buy this in many Italian markets and health food stores)

½ teaspoon salt

8 tablespoons (1 stick) unsalted butter, softened

1 teaspoon grated orange zest

One 15-ounce container ricotta

4 large eggs

⅔ cup sugar

3 tablespoons orange flower water or fresh orange juice

1 teaspoon ground cinnamon

½ cup very finely chopped candied citron

½ cup very finely chopped candied orange peel

DOUGH

12 tablespoons (1½ sticks) unsalted butter, at room temperature

1 cup confectioners' sugar

1 large egg

2 large egg yolks

1 teaspoon grated orange zest

3 cups all-purpose flour

½ teaspoon ground cinnamon

½ teaspoon salt

1 egg yolk, beaten with 1 tablespoon water

Confectioners' sugar

PREPARATION

For the filling, soak the wheat in cold water to cover. Refrigerate overnight.

The next day, drain the wheat and place it in a medium saucepan with fresh cold water to cover. Add the salt and bring to a simmer over medium heat. Cook, stirring occasionally, until the wheat is tender, 20 to 30 minutes.

Drain the wheat and place in a large bowl. Stir in the butter and orange zest until the butter melts. Let cool.

In a large bowl, beat together the ricotta, eggs, sugar, orange flower water, and cinnamon. Stir in the wheat mixture and candied fruits. Cover and refrigerate until ready to use.

To make the dough, in a large mixer bowl, beat the butter and confectioners' sugar until light and fluffy. Add the egg and yolks and beat until smooth. Beat in the orange zest. Add the flour, cinnamon, and salt and mix just until a dough forms. If the dough seems dry, add a spoonful or two of ice water.

Shape one-quarter of the dough into a disk. Make a second disk with the remaining dough. Wrap each piece in plastic wrap and chill 1 hour, or overnight.

Preheat the oven to 350°F. Butter and flour a 9 x 3-inch springform pan. Tap out the excess flour.

Roll out the larger piece of dough to a 15-inch circle. Drape the dough over the rolling pin and, using the pin to lift it, fit the dough into the pan, flattening out any wrinkles against the inside of the pan. Scrape the filling into the pan.

Roll out the smaller piece of dough to a 10-inch circle. Cut the dough into ½-inch-wide strips. Lay half the strips 1 inch apart across the filling. Turn the pan clockwise and place the remaining strips on top, forming a lattice pattern. Press the ends of the strips against the dough on the sides of the pan. Trim the dough and press firmly to seal. Brush the dough with the beaten egg.

Bake 1 hour and 10 minutes, or until the pie is golden brown on top and the filling is puffed. Let the pie cool in the pan on a rack 15 minutes.

Remove the sides of the pan and let the pie cool completely, then cover and refrigerate at least overnight. (The pie can be stored in the refrigerator up to 3 days.) Just before serving, sprinkle the pie with confectioners' sugar.

EASTER SWEET BREAD

Makes 2 round loaves

INGREDIENTS

8 tablespoons (1 stick) unsalted butter

½ cup milk

1 envelope (2½ teaspoons) active dry yeast

½ cup warm water (100° to 110°F)

3 large eggs, at room temperature

⅔ cup sugar

1 teaspoon vanilla

1 tablespoon grated orange zest

About 5 cups all-purpose flour

1 teaspoon salt

6 eggs, colored for Easter, if desired

1 egg yolk, beaten with 1 tablespoon water

Multicolored round candy sprinkles

PREPARATION

Heat the butter with the milk in a small saucepan just until the butter melts. Let cool.

Sprinkle the yeast over the warm water. Let stand until the yeast is creamy, about 5 minutes. Stir until dissolved.

In a large mixer bowl, beat the 3 eggs until foamy. Beat in the sugar until blended. Add the butter mixture, yeast, vanilla, and orange zest. Add 4½ cups of the flour and the salt, mixing until a soft dough forms. Gradually add just enough of the remaining flour to make a smooth, slightly sticky dough.

Turn the dough out onto a lightly floured surface and knead it for a minute or so, until it is very smooth. Shape the dough into a ball.

Butter a large bowl and place the dough in it. Cover with plastic wrap and let rise in a warm place until doubled in volume, about 1½ hours.

Butter two large baking sheets. Punch down the dough and cut it into 4 pieces. Roll out one piece between your hands into a rope about 22 inches long. Repeat with another piece of dough. Lay the ropes side by side and loosely braid them together. Lift the braid onto one of the prepared baking sheets and bring the ends together to form a ring. Pinch the ends to seal. Place 3 of the whole eggs at intervals around the wreath, tucking them in between the ropes of the dough. Repeat with the remaining dough and eggs. Cover with plastic wrap and let rise about 45 minutes, until doubled in size.

Preheat the oven to 350°F.

Brush the dough with the egg yolk mixture. Scatter the candy sprinkles on top. Bake for about 30 minutes, or until golden brown, reversing the position of the pans halfway through the baking time. Transfer the bread to racks to cool completely.

Cut into slices to serve. (Nobody ever eats the eggs, but store the bread in the refrigerator just in case.)

Chapter 7

SMALL EVENTS FOR WOMEN ONLY

Okay, that's enough of the big, complicated three-weeks-in-the-planning-style dinners, banquets, and family reunions for a while. Let's turn our attention to something we all enjoy, or long to enjoy, as an important and revitalizing ritual in our lives—small parties for women only.

Speaking for myself, I have a husband who is a very big presence in our household, not to mention a son on the cusp between boyhood and manhood. As my sister-in-law, Janice, once expressed to me in a fit of rage (and I've cleaned this up considerably), Italian-American men tend to be "swaggering mama's boys, [blank] hypocrites . . . emotional cripples . . . and they expect their wives to live like the [blank] nuns of Mount Carmel College." Now, I think that assessment is a bit harsh, and perhaps mirrors Janice's particular frustration with men at the moment, but there's a grain of truth in there somewhere. Italian men do seem to lean on their mothers for emotional support, and when their mothers fail them or pass on, their wives often take up the burden. It's safe to say that modern men of all stripes are time-consuming and often depend heavily on their wives and girlfriends for everything from clean socks to wiping away the tears of professional agony and failure. We love them and we forgive them for their many childish out-

bursts and demands, but sanity dictates that we escape their presence whenever we can.

When women are around just women, two things happen, I think. One, they take each other and each other's thoughts more seriously. Men tend to talk loud and want the last word, which is why they aren't invited. Two, women with women can act as girly or non-girly as they wish. They can wear frilly hats and organza dresses, decorate in baby pink and baby blue, and hand out delicate bath soaps as party favors. They can make an ornate place card in pink calligraphy. They can, in a word, indulge themselves.

I decided to call in some of my dearest friends to help me expand on the subject of small women-only affairs. Most of these women I have known since high school, and we've gathered in dozens of different ways over the years to watch films, discuss books, raise money for hospitals and churches, or just to have lunch and let our collective hair down. (Our group

MUSIC ♪

Soundtrack from *A Room with a View*. Soundtrack from *Out of Africa*. Anything from Celine Dion. Soundtrack from *Remains of the Day*. In other words, your favorite movie soundtrack.

doesn't play bridge or mah-jongg, but if we did, I'm sure that would be fun too.) Some of us have had husbands who have passed away; others, unfortunately, still have them around to complain about. (Just kidding!) Our circle is pretty tight after so many years of personal ups and downs, and we seldom invite a new person to join the club. That may be a vice, not a virtue—new people often broaden your interests and help you discover new things about yourself—but the warmth and security of a set group of old girlfriends is not to be minimized. Perhaps this is merely the tendency of Italian-Americans, male and female, to stick

HOW TO LEAD A BOOK OR FILM CLUB

• Take charge. To get such a group going from scratch, invite a congenial list of likeminded friends and query them by phone about a book or film choice. Make it enticing—choose a book or film that everyone wants to read or see, not something they *should* read or see.

• Do a little research and pass it on. If the book is, say, *The Da Vinci Code*, pass around a few articles about the controversy surrounding the book. It's easy to do this via e-mail, if you can do that. Regular mail always works too. There are over three thousand reader reviews of *The Da Vinci Code* on Amazon. Read a few of them.

• Be ready to lead the discussion. In fact, pick a discussion leader for each time you meet. At least you'll know that one person has read the book and thought about it. Often a book discussion begins with what exactly happened in the book and some key factual elements. What is Opus Dei, anyway? Again, a little research can add a lot.

• A good book usually has passages that are great to read out loud to get a real sense of the style and attitude of the writer. Pick out a passage or two that really struck you and read them to your friends. Seriously. That's probably the part of the book they'll remember the longest.

• Plant a ringer, i.e., one participant you know will weigh in with a considered opinion or some relevant information when needed. If no one is willing to step up and be a little more prepared than the others, your book club may be in trouble.

• If it's not a full-blown lunch, add the element of a coffee or tea party to the affair. Even if people are screaming at each other over the book or film, they'll quiet down to eat a delicious cannoli or other such delicacy.

• Finally, have a list of books to choose from for next time. Just a discussion *about* books could turn out to be a good discussion *of* books.

closely to their own, but for all I know, it's also the tendency of Irish-Americans, Korean-Americans, and Baptist-Americans too.

Briefly, "our group" includes: Rosalie Aprile, a widow whose late husband was my husband's dearest friend in the world; Gabriella Dante, whose husband is a local club owner and business associate of my hus-

band; Helen Barone, another wife of a business associate of my husband; and my husband's sister, the aforementioned Janice Soprano Baccilieri. Sadly, two long-time members of our cluster, Karen Baccilieri and Adriana La Cerva, are no longer with us, for various reasons. Nevertheless, they are with us in our hearts at every luncheon or church rummage sale.

We gathered at my house midmorning, and because of lovely weather, sat out by the pool. Coffee and Italian pastries were served.

Carmela: Okay, let's take a vote. Which do we prefer when we get together in each other's home for whatever reason—buffet or sit-down?

Janice: I prefer eating at Vesuvio's and let Artie worry about the place settings.

Carmela: Of course, because no one has to do any work, but home is more personal, don't you think?

Gabriella: Okay, for me, I like the idea of a sit-down, white-glove–type luncheon with all the frills, almost like we were playing dress-up as little kids. The table should have a white lace or satin tablecloth, in other words, good linen, with the best wineglasses and the best china in the house. Even including charger plates.

CARMELA'S **10** FAVORITE ALL-TIME ALL-WOMEN PARTY GIFTS

1 A ceramic angel.

2 A group portrait, taken at the last get-together, nicely framed for each member of "the group."

3 A beaded pillbox.

4 A book of daily affirmations.

5 A large velvet pillow with beaded tassels, placed under each setting at a sit-down luncheon, in lieu of a placemat or charger plate.

6 A small monogrammed photo album.

7 A satin drawstring bag for storing lingerie.

8 Scented bath salts or a small bottle of exquisite bath oil.

9 A silver-plated heart-shaped compact.

10 For a very special occasion—like a reunion of a small group of old friends or the occasion of one of the group moving away or passing away—a commemorative poem written by the hostess.

Rosalie: Okay, I'm stupid, but what is a charger plate?

Gabriella: It's a very nice, big decorative plate that you put under the plates with the food. It protects the linens from, say, a plate with pasta falling off the sides. Plus, it adds a touch of refinement, if you know what I mean.

Rosalie: I always wondered what those things were called. Yes, definitely, let's have those.

Gabriella: I've seen charger plates in the catalogs that are gold, silver, even pastel pink. Actually, when I stop to think, they could set up the whole look of the table, right?

Carmela: You know what a calla lily is? It's a sculptured flower that comes in all kinds of colors, including a rosy pink. Can each pink charger plate have a small bouquet of pink calla lilies next to it?

Gabriella: Sure, have all the flowers you want. I'd like a big glass candelabra in the middle of the table and surrounding it, maybe five or six small round vases filled with pink and white peonies.

Janice: More pink. I see a trend. What are we drinking at this hoity-toity lunch?

Helen: Wine, maybe, if you know what wine goes with what food, which I don't. And champagne, of course. I like it when people add a little something to each champagne glass.

Janice: Something pink?

Carmela: Champagne "flute," to be exact.

Helen: Right, flute. (Jots it down on a pad.) Anyway, in each flute, add a few fresh little raspberries, for instance. Or maybe a little rose blossom with a little toothpick running through it. Isn't that sweet?

Janice: Terribly. Now here's something I saw on the Food Channel that I thought was really cool. Take a bottle of vodka and serve it encased in a mold of frozen flowers.

Karen, Our Friend
by Carmela Soprano

We have so few friends in our life
Yet we take them all for granted
Then one dies, like the cut of a knife
And we know they can't be supplanted.

Rosie is here, and Gabby is there,
Though they've both had their measure of strife.
But Karen, sweet Karen, her death a nightmare
And her sin? To be a good wife.

I'm bitter, I'm mad, I'm heartbroken, I'm sad,
What God would do something so hateful?
The only lesson here I see to be had,
The only good thought here I think I can add,
Is to quit our complaining, our whining and waning,
And for all of our friends, be ever grateful.

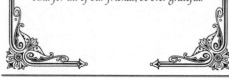

Carmela: And how do you do that?

Janice: Easy. You might want to take notes. You get an empty milk carton, a big one, cut the top off and stick the bottle inside. Then add rose petals or the like around it, pour water to cover those, then more petals and water until you're at the top. Then freeze the whole thing. When it's hard as a rock, you cut away the milk carton, place it on a tray, and ta-da, you have frozen vodka in flowers.

Rosalie: Sounds like a lot of work.

Helen: Sounds like a fun way to have lunch to me.

Gabriella: So, there you have it. (Checking her notes.) A beautiful white linen table setting with pink charger plates, fine china, a candelabra in the middle, pink calla lilies, either champagne with raspberries in champagne *flutes* or vodka in frozen flowers. Sounds lovely. Whose house and when?

Janice: Wait. What are we eating at this "Ladies Who Lunch" lunch?

Rosalie: Oh, I don't know, what about . . . (reels off the menu) . . . *Mozzarel'* in Carozza, Chicken Paillards, Baked Asparagus and Prosciutto Rolls, and a nice Gelato Affogato for dessert.

Janice: That's perfect! Did you just come up with that off the top of your head?

Rosalie: No, I started writing down ideas way back at the charger plates.

Carmela: You know, we should do this regularly: have a luncheon to discuss all the decorating and entertaining details for another luncheon. Along with the book club and the film club and the St. Peter and Paul's African Relief Lunch, we'll have a regular entertaining lunch.

Janice: Good. Let's eat some pastries.

NAPKIN FOLDING by Gabriella Dante

Gabby took a course at the West Orange Arts & Crafts Center on the art of napkin folding and insisted on passing some of her techniques to the rest of us. *CS*

Napkin Folding

Folded napkin beautiful thing = beautiful food arrange.
Like sushi at Japanese place. Don't have to eat raw fish — yuck! — to admire the delicate food on plate design.
Elegantly folded nap something you see at Four Seasons. You can do it!
Easier than you think.

Start with starched square dinner napkin. Like 16 by 16. Pretty big.

16"

16"

Three basic folds:

① Fleur-de-Lis. Means "Flower of the Lily." Use a napkin ring.
Spread napkin on flat surface, fold in half horizontally. Crease at bottom.
Fold upper right to center of napk. Fold upper left to center of napk.

Now have TRIANGLE!

Fold lower right corner up to center. Repeat with lower left.

Now have shape of DIAMOND!

Now fold and flare top points out slightly = like wings.
Slip bottom of napk into ring. That's it.

② Symphony Fold. Use with napkin ring. Spread napkin on flat surface.
Fold napkin into thirds, with the open edge at the bottom.
Then roll upper right and upper left corners diagonally toward center.

Two cone shapes will form from rolling.

Then turn upside down — open end now up —
and stick in a champagne flute.

Dramatic!

③ Taper Roll. Freestanding. Looks like a taper candle. Spread napkin on flat surface.

Like always.

Fold napk in half to create a triangle, with crease at bottom.
Fold up bottom edge to make CUFF. Flip napk over.
Very tightly, roll the napk from right to left.
Tuck left corner into cuff.
Stand upright on plate.

=

☆ Note to self. Remember, you can do it. Keep trying.

PU Sil's suit at cleaners!

MOZZARELLA IN CAROZZA

Toasted Mozzarella Sandwiches

Serves 4 to 8

INGREDIENTS

SAUCE

3 tablespoons unsalted butter

1 tablespoon olive oil

6 anchovy fillets, chopped

1 tablespoon fresh lemon juice

SANDWICHES

4 ounces fresh mozzarella, cut into 4 slices

8 slices good-quality white bread, crusts removed

¾ cup milk

⅓ cup all-purpose flour

2 eggs

1 tablespoon water

About 1 tablespoon unsalted butter

1 tablespoon chopped fresh flat-leaf parsley

PREPARATION

To make the sauce, melt the butter with the oil and anchovies in a small saucepan. Swirl in the lemon juice. Cover and keep warm.

To make the sandwiches, place a slice of cheese between two slices of bread. Repeat with the remaining cheese and bread. Pour the milk into a shallow dish. Spread the flour on a piece of wax paper. In another dish, beat the eggs with the water.

Melt ½ tablespoon of the butter on a griddle or in a large skillet over medium heat. Lightly dip each sandwich on both sides first in the milk, then in the flour, and finally in the eggs. Place in the pan and cook the first side until golden, about 4 minutes, flattening the sandwiches with a pancake turner. Flip the sandwiches over and add a little more butter, if needed. Cook until the sandwiches are golden and the cheese is melting.

Cut the sandwiches into quarters on the diagonal. Place them, overlapping slightly, on a warm serving platter. Pour the sauce over the sandwiches. Sprinkle with the parsley and serve immediately.

CHICKEN PAILLARDS WITH TOMATO-OLIVE SALAD

Serves 4

INGREDIENTS

4 boneless, skinless chicken breast halves

2 tablespoons olive oil

1 tablespoon chopped fresh thyme or basil

Salt and freshly ground pepper

SALAD

2 tablespoons extra virgin olive oil

1 tablespoon balsamic vinegar

Salt and freshly ground pepper

6 cups mesclun or baby salad greens, rinsed and well dried

2 ripe medium tomatoes, diced

½ cup black olives, such as Gaeta, pitted and coarsely chopped

PREPARATION

Place a chicken breast between two sheets of plastic wrap and gently pound the chicken until it is about ¼ inch thick. Repeat with the remaining chicken. Place the pieces in a bowl and toss them with the oil, thyme, and salt and pepper to taste.

In a large salad bowl, whisk together the oil, vinegar, and salt and pepper to taste.

Brush a large grill pan or nonstick skillet with oil. Heat the pan over medium-high heat. Arrange the chicken pieces on the pan and cook 4 to 5 minutes, or until the chicken is nicely browned on the first side. Turn the pieces and cook 2 minutes more, or until cooked through.

Arrange the chicken on four plates. Toss the greens, tomatoes, and olives with the dressing. Place the salad on top of the chicken and serve immediately.

ASPARAGUS AND PROSCIUTTO ROLLS

Serves 6

INGREDIENTS

18 thick asparagus spears, trimmed

2 teaspoons salt

6 slices imported Italian prosciutto, such as prosciutto di Parma

4 ounces Fontina, cut into thin slices

2 tablespoons unsalted butter, melted

Freshly ground pepper

PREPARATION

Bring about 2 inches of water to a boil in a large shallow pan. Add the asparagus and salt and cook until the asparagus are partially tender when pierced with a fork, about 4 minutes, depending on their thickness. Drain the asparagus and rinse them under cool water. Pat dry.

Preheat the oven to 350°F. Butter a large baking dish.

Make 6 bundles of 3 asparagus each. Wrap a slice of prosciutto around the center of each bundle. Place the bundles in the baking dish. Lay the pieces of cheese on top of the prosciutto. Brush the butter over the asparagus. Sprinkle with pepper.

Bake 15 minutes, or until the cheese is melted and the asparagus are tender. Serve hot.

ANISETTE TOASTS

Makes about 50

INGREDIENTS

3 cups all-purpose flour

½ cup cornstarch

1 tablespoon baking powder

½ teaspoon salt

6 large eggs

1½ cups sugar

1 tablespoon anise extract

PREPARATION

Preheat the oven to 400°F. Butter a 13 x 9 x 2-inch baking pan.

Sift together the dry ingredients onto a piece of wax paper.

In a large mixer bowl, beat the eggs until foamy. Add the sugar about a tablespoon at a time, beating constantly until very light and fluffy. Beat in the anise extract. With a rubber spatula, gradually fold in the dry ingredients just until blended.

Scrape the mixture into the prepared pan and spread it out evenly. Bake 20 to 22 minutes, or until the top is golden and a toothpick inserted in the center comes out clean. Remove the pan from the oven but leave the oven on.

Let the cake cool for 5 minutes, then invert it onto a cutting board. With a serrated knife, cut the cake lengthwise in half. Cut each half crosswise into ½-inch-thick slices.

Place the slices in a single layer on two large baking sheets. Bake for 10 to 12 minutes, or until the cookies are toasted and crisp. Transfer to racks to cool.

Store in an airtight container. These keep a long time.

GELATO AFFOGATO

"Drowned" Ice Cream

Serves 6

INGREDIENTS

About 2 pints coffee (or another flavor) premium ice cream

1 cup hot espresso

3 tablespoons dark rum

PREPARATION

Scoop the ice cream into six small coffee cups or goblets.

Stir together the hot coffee and rum. Slowly pour the coffee over the ice cream. Serve immediately.

Chapter 8

SMALL EVENTS FOR MEN ONLY

What do I know about how men like to be entertained, especially when they are among themselves and don't want my gender around? I take dinner orders from men on a daily basis, and I know how to fill the refrigerator when they wander in and plop down in our media room to watch a football game, but beyond that, I don't really follow their creative "entertaining" ideas and tastes. In general, I don't think they have any such ideas or tastes. I have never once seen my husband rummaging through *GQ* or the Sharper Image catalog, looking for ways to dress up his next poker game or Super Bowl party. He has specific items that he will spend endless hours researching and pontificating about—cigars, single-malt Scotch, who makes the best flat-screen, hi-def, wall-mounted TV, which Patek-Philippe watch is his next heirloom, etc.—but he doesn't give a hoot if the napkins at the party are folded in fleur-de-lis or symphony style. If you invited him to a six-course gourmet dinner for twelve with fine china and charger plates, he'd say, "Hey, this is nice, what's this fork for?" and start eating.

Have you ever heard the term "metrosexual"? Me neither, until they were discussing it on *The View* one day and I just happened to

be by a TV. A metrosexual is a man, I guess, who isn't gay but likes some of the finer things in life that women tend to like, like a good facial exfoliant or a color-coordinated buffet table. Well, I'm not talking about those kind of men here. I've met a few "metros" at large charity functions, but none of them would last long around my husband and his less polished friends. My husband's group can dress very nicely, and often do. They like to take saunas, get massages, have a professional manicure, and style their hair in an often unique, personality-defining fashion. But their love of social aesthetics pretty much stops there. They could care less about their entertaining *surroundings*, whether at a Sunday buffet or a wake for their mother. If the furniture is comfortable and the food, plentiful, they're happy. Color schemes? Black. Black is generally style-proof for any occasion.

But men, like women, need their time alone, away from the stresses and strains of domestic life, and if my husband is any indication, they are not bashful in demanding this time. Sometimes it feels like he and his clique of buddies never left high school. They seem to feel most comfortable when they are busting each other's chops and/or going on escapades together, like a trip to an Indian casino up north or a Saturday night "business" meeting in New York. Have you ever seen a group of high

school boys cursing and roughhousing while stuffing their mouths at the pizza parlor? That's my husband and his friends, except they're stuffing their mouths with pepper and egg sandwiches in the back of Satriale's Pork Store.

But what do they think about, if anything, when they are planning an all-male affair? I asked perhaps the most thoughtful of the group, Peter Paul ("Paulie Walnuts") Gualtieri, for some perspective. Here's what he said into my trusty tape recorder:

"Thank you, Carmela, for this opportunity to speak of something of which I know. When it comes to entertaining, men, you see, are more interested in the activity at hand rather than the room or table décor. But don't get me wrong. It's not that you can just plant a bunch of guys in an empty warehouse or a lady's pink boudoir and think they are so oblivious that they can settle in with no concern for the setting. It's not that we don't care where we are or the décor we are in; it's just that we care about different things. This is only natural. You care about the poinsettia plants and the little napkins that say 'You Finally Did It!' We care about what we care about, whether we're in mixed company or just amongst ourselves. It makes no difference, really.

"Personally, I live alone, at least for now, so the company of my fellow friends is important to my particular situation. I look after my mother, Nucci, but that's different. When it comes to the general layout of an all-male gathering, like say, a friendly night of cards and laughter, I, for one, insist on cleanliness. And I think I speak for many men when I say this. It is a gross misnomer that men are germ-infested slobs like the filthy guy on *The Odd Couple*. Of course they're not pansies like the other guy,

MUSIC ♪

Dino. End of conversation.

A SHORT COURSE ON EXPENSIVE CIGARS
by Bobby Bacala

I am no *Jeopardy!*-level expert on cigars, but I have many friends who are yet wish to remain anonymous because of the current legal situation with Cuba. Like the magazine of the same name, they are true "aficionados"; these tips were collected from them, along with some light reading I did on the subject. You could take a college course on cigars. I'm just giving you a few starters. Thank you.

• The only cigars worth smoking are handmade. They have a completely sealed end that needs clipping. The rest are garbage.

• Like all tobacco, cigars should be fresh. Here's a quick test: Roll the cigar between your fingers. If it's lumpy or mushy, or if the outer layer of tobacco, or wrapper, is crackled or rippled, it's probably old. A good cigar should feel firm to the touch, be uniform in color, and have a smooth, oily wrapper.

• The pros say: The ash should be white, indicating the tobacco was grown in good soil. The burn should be slow and even. An uneven burn is not only a mess, it can affect the often complex taste of a good cigar.

• The color of the wrapper indicates a cigar's flavor. Many new smokers find the darker, or "maduro," wrappers too harsh and lean toward the lighter wrappers, sometimes called "natural," "claro," or "English market selection."

• Learn a little about size before you head to the cigar store. A cigar is measured by ring gauge and length. A 64-ring cigar may be an inch in diameter, i.e., a big one. The classic mid-range size is the "corona," which is between 5 and 6 inches long and has a ring gauge of about 40. It takes 30 to 40 minutes to smoke one. Two other size names to remember: the "robusto," short and fat, 48 to 50 ring, and 4 inches long. And the "Churchill," large like the man, 7 to 8 inches long, and a ring gauge of 48 to 50. Allot yourself an hour to smoke one of those. What's the right size for you? How would I know? I don't know you.

• Cubans. The country of origin is important. Cuban cigars, considered the world's best, at least by Fidel Castro, are illegal to sell in the States, and may no longer be the world's best, according to some. *"Hecho en Cuba"* (made in Cuba) used to mean quality and consistency; now it's not always the case. The best way to purchase Cubans is to buy and smoke them in Canada or Europe, but watch out for fakes (look for the large Cuban tax stamp on the box). If you want to bring some home, throw away the bands and box and no one will know the difference, but you didn't get that from me.

• Non-Cubans. If you want to stay within the law, you'll probably go with Dominican cigars, maybe Jamaican, considered mild, or Honduran, if you want a stronger taste. Mexican and Nicaraguan fall in between. There are brand names, of course, that generally deliver the goods: Macanudo, Don Diego, CAO, Davidoff, or H. Upmann, to name a few and with no disrespect for the many others.

• You pay what you pay. Currently, in my area, a box of high-quality Arturo Fuente Hemingways can run you about $175. Of course, don't buy a box until you're sure you want to smoke a box and have the right moisture conditions to store a box. Ask your cigar man about this. Storage is too big to discuss here.

• To properly light a cigar, keep the flame from touching the tip (which you've learned to cut off properly) and use a sulfur-free lighting source, if possible. Once you got it going with a few big puffs and need a break from smoking, park it in an ashtray deep enough to hold the ashes without the cigar tip resting on the tray. Otherwise, the cigar will burn unevenly or go out altogether, and you don't want that.

POKER ETIQUETTE
by Silvio Dante

I am a big stickler when it comes to proper card game etiquette. The slightest breach, as it were, can destroy my concentration and create dissent among the players. Just follow these don'ts, okay?

1 *Don't* play slowly. Nothing ruins a game faster than one moron who thinks this is quantum physics and needs twenty minutes to do the math. It's not quantum anything. Make a decision and get on with it.

2 *Don't* clean. I have been known to lose my temper at the sight of some lackey cleaning cheese off the floor around my feet in the middle of a game. Don't sweep, vacuum, empty ashtrays, or Lemon Pledge during a game. If that's your job, be very careful.

3 *Don't* forget what's going on. "Hey, is it my turn?" "What did he just do?" "What are we playing again?" One too many of those, and you're back on the street. If you act out of turn because you don't know what's happening or simply because you're an idiot, like tossing your cards as soon as they're dealt—don't do that, either.

4 *Don't* talk too much, especially about the cards. Something like, "Hey, that's a diamond, he could have a flush," or "I'm not in but I'd get out if I were you," could get you in real trouble.

5 *Don't* "splash" the pot with your chips like you're throwing sunflower seeds to a pigeon. And don't take your chips off the table at any time during a game. Both practices are obnoxious and won't be tolerated.

6 *Don't* ever ask for assistance from another player. This is a mark of a rank amateur but, unfortunately, goes on more than you think. It usually comes from a newcomer, as in, "You know these guys, Sil, do you think this hand can beat them?" If confronted with such a person, always give them explicit money-losing advice. They'll learn fast.

7 *Don't* be a poor winner. Tip the dealer, for sure, and don't keep stacking and restacking your big load of chips like you were Donald Trump building a skyscraper. Lose any way you want, as long as you pay up, but win with class.

either. If I walk into a club-style room, even if it's a temporary arrangement in an empty office or apartment, it must be clean and well-organized, or my comfort level goes way down.

"Cleanliness is not always hard work, you know. For instance, it's a little known but useful fact that, in a jam, you can quickly clean a toilet using nothing but two Alka-Seltzer tablets and a can of Coke. Same fast-acting fizz as a commercial cleaner. And how hard is it to take a paper towel and a little spray cleaner and wipe off a table before laying a piece of felt on it? Not very.

"Well-organized means having the key essentials on hand that make for a good time. Every *useful* thing in its place, I say. The ice is more important than the tablecloth, if you catch my drift. Matches and ashtrays, of course, and maybe one of those little hand fans for blowing the smoke away if it gets too thick. Corkscrews, can openers, toothpicks, a knife sharp enough to cut an apple, a clean bathroom with antibacterial soap—these are the kinds of the things that can make or break a male gathering. I'm not going to walk you through every last one of them, because you're smart enough to make your own list. Some of your friends might even require a spittoon, I don't know.

"It's the little details that count. If there will be drinking, have an ample supply of aspirin, perhaps an effervescent antacid, and plenty of hot coffee on hand. If you don't get a headache from cigar smoke or an upset stomach from spicy foods, maybe one of your guests does. How much better will he feel if you hand him two extra-strength aspirins just as he's in the middle of a losing streak? It could make his whole night.

"Beyond that, have the right equipment for the occasion. If it's gambling, don't be cheap and buy the little plastic chips from the hobby shop. Imagine the chips they play with in AC or Vegas and try to get close to that. All decks of cards, of course, should be unopened, even if it's just a friendly game in the garage. You can get fancy and find cards with 'Caesar's' or naked girls on them, but I could care less. If the cards are unopened and of a high quality, they could have Jimmy Carter's face on them for all I care.

"If your affair calls for a stripper, like, say, for a bachelor's party or for halftime at a Super Bowl viewing, go with a professional and go with a personal recommendation from a friend if possible. If you or a trustworthy acquaintance frequents a reputable strip club, start there. If you go to a web site or an ad in one of those throwaway 'Outcall Massage' newspapers, you're on your own and you'll probably get burned. First, you'll get an answering machine (use a false name) and the 'Are you serious?' runaround. The stripper, if she shows up at all after your credit card 'prepayment,' will be flabby and misshapen, the price will suddenly double, and her 'boyfriend' will ensure you get to see her gifts for all of twelve minutes. Or, per her ruse, it's all about a group back massage until someone mentions something lewd and the stripper turns out to be a cop.

"It's perfectly okay for a pro to bring along a male body guard. It's common practice. If she brings along sixteen low-riders in oversized white T-shirts and stocking caps, you may have chosen a disreputable female entertainer. In general, if you've had no experience in such matters, maybe you should consult someone in your area who has.

"A parting word about food and food preparation. In the tradition I come from, men cook, and cook enthusiastically. In fact, we sometimes have as much fun cooking together as we do being together at the event which we are cooking for. Cooking and eating becomes an essential part of this event, a group activity that can breed friendliness and trust,

grappa

Grappa originated in Italy's Veneto region in the fifth century and is actually a type of brandy. It is extracted from all the leftovers of the wine-making process— the grape skins, stems, seeds, pulp, even an occasional bug. For centuries it was only locally made and locally consumed, a way for farmers to wring the last little something out of every grape. It was a coarse, stomach-burning country drink that one expert called "little more than a cheap, portable form of central heating for peasants of Northern Italy." It's strong and can give you a serious hangover, but a small shot in your morning coffee can get you going fast.

Today's commercial grappa is gentler, smoother, more sophisticated, and more expensive, a drink growers hope will appeal to a worldwide audience of Cognac or whiskey drinkers. Along with higher-grade leftovers as a primary source, growers now add fruits, nuts, and herbs to the mix and package grappa in exotic, strangely shaped colored bottles. Grappa is best consumed after dinner, either alone or with coffee or espresso. Sometimes, the specially-made grappa glasses are chilled to lessen the initial bite. In any case, let it breathe in the glass for three to five minutes. If you really like the taste, try a little in your breakfast coffee. Many do.

whether the occasion be business or pleasure. If you have a weekly card game, maybe one guy could be designated each week to either cook something up or at least pick something up at a reputable deli in the area. I knew these guys once who got together regularly and had one guy who always came and whipped up a delicious meal. Once done, he took off to hang out with his mistress while his buddies covered for him. The wife might call and they'd say, 'He just left,' or 'He's in the john,' then call the guy and alert him. This went on for years, and all because the man could cook. I rest my case."

CAPONATA

Sweet-and-Sour Eggplant

Serves 6

INGREDIENTS

1 large eggplant (about 1¼ pounds), cut into 1-inch dice

Salt

1 large onion, chopped

1½ cups chopped celery

¼ cup olive oil

1½ cups chopped canned tomatoes

1 cup chopped green olives

¼ cup capers, rinsed and drained

3 tablespoons sugar

⅓ cup red wine vinegar

Vegetable oil for frying

PREPARATION

Layer the eggplant in a colander, sprinkling each layer with salt. Place the colander over a plate and let stand 1 hour to drain.

In a large saucepan, cook the onion and celery in the olive oil over medium heat until softened, about 5 minutes. Add the tomatoes, bring to a simmer, and cook 15 minutes. Stir in the olives, capers, sugar, and vinegar. Bring to a simmer and cook 5 minutes more. Remove from the heat.

Rinse the eggplant pieces and pat dry with paper towels. In a large heavy skillet, heat ½ inch of vegetable oil over medium-high until a small piece of eggplant sizzles rapidly when added. Being careful not to splash the oil, add as much of the eggplant as will fit in the pan without crowding. Cook, stirring frequently, until golden brown, about 10 minutes. Remove the eggplant with a slotted spoon and drain on paper towels. Cook the remaining eggplant in the same way.

Stir the eggplant into the tomato sauce and simmer 10 minutes. Let cool to room temperature before serving. (Caponata can be stored in the refrigerator up to 3 days.)

PROSCIUTTO BREAD

Serves 8 to 10

INGREDIENTS

2 packages (2½ teaspoons each) active dry yeast

1½ cups warm water (100° to 110°F)

3 tablespoons olive oil

About 3½ cups unbleached all-purpose flour

1 teaspoon salt

1 teaspoon coarsely ground black pepper

4 ounces prosciutto, in one thick slice, cut into small dice

4 ounces soppressata or other salami, diced

2 ounces sharp provolone, cut into small dice

PREPARATION

In a small bowl, sprinkle the yeast over warm water. Let stand 5 minutes or until creamy. Stir until the yeast is dissolved.

In a large mixer bowl or in a food processor, combine 3½ cups flour, the salt, and pepper. Add the yeast and oil. Mix or process until the dough comes together and forms a ball. Remove the dough from the bowl and knead 1 minute, or until smooth. Add more flour if necessary until the dough feels moist but no longer sticky.

Oil a large bowl. Add the dough, turning it once to coat the top. Cover with plastic wrap and let rise in a warm place until doubled in volume, about 1 hour.

Oil a large baking sheet. Place the dough on a lightly floured surface and flatten it with your

hands to eliminate air bubbles. Scatter the prosciutto, soppressata, and cheese over the surface. Fold the dough over to enclose the meat and cheese, then flatten and fold the dough several times to distribute the ingredients evenly.

Cut the dough in half. Roll each piece between your palms into a 10-inch loaf. Place the loaves several inches apart on the baking sheets. Cover and let rise until doubled, about 1 hour.

Preheat the oven to 400°F.

With a sharp knife, cut 3 diagonal slashes in each loaf. Bake for 30 minutes, or until golden brown. Slide the bread onto a wire rack to cool slightly. Serve warm.

STUFFED HOT CHERRY PEPPERS

Serves 8

INGREDIENTS

One 32-ounce jar pickled red and green hot cherry peppers

One 2-ounce can anchovy fillets, drained

1 garlic clove, minced

1 cup plain dry bread crumbs, preferably homemade from Italian bread

2 tablespoons capers, very finely chopped

About 3 tablespoons extra virgin olive oil

PREPARATION

Drain the peppers, reserving the liquid. Cut off the tops of the peppers. With a demitasse spoon, scoop out the seeds. (You might want to wear rubber gloves while handling these peppers.)

In a small bowl, mash the anchovies and garlic. Add the bread crumbs, capers, 3 tablespoons oil, and 1 to 2 tablespoons of the reserved pepper liquid. Mix well, adding a little more oil if needed to moisten the crumbs.

Stuff the peppers with the bread crumb mixture, pressing it in lightly. Refrigerate up to 5 days.

Just before serving, drizzle the peppers with a little more olive oil.

FRIED MOZZARELLA STICKS

Serves 6

INGREDIENTS

1 pound fresh mozzarella

3 large eggs, beaten

½ teaspoon salt

¼ teaspoon freshly ground pepper

½ cup all-purpose flour

1 cup plain dry bread crumbs, preferably homemade from Italian bread

Vegetable oil for frying

Tomato Sauce (page 32; optional)

PREPARATION

Cut the mozzarella into ½-inch slices. Cut the slices into ½-inch-wide sticks. Pat the pieces dry with paper towels.

In a shallow plate, beat the eggs with the salt and pepper. Spread the flour on a piece of wax paper. Spread the bread crumbs on another piece of wax paper.

Dip the cheese sticks first in the egg, then roll them in the flour, then dip again in the egg, and finally roll them in the bread crumbs. Make sure they are completely coated and sealed in with the eggs and crumbs. Place the sticks on a rack and refrigerate them for 30 minutes, or overnight, to set.

Pour about 1 inch of oil into a deep heavy skillet. Heat over medium-high heat until very hot. Add only as many of the mozzarella sticks as will fit comfortably without crowding the pan and fry, turning the pieces carefully, until browned on all sides, about 5 minutes. Drain on paper towels. Fry the remaining sticks in the same way.

Serve hot, plain or with the tomato sauce.

SAUSAGE, PEPPER, AND ONION HEROES

Serves 4

INGREDIENTS

4 Italian-style pork sausages
3 tablespoons olive oil
2 bell peppers, preferably 1 red and 1 green, cored, seeded, and cut into ½-inch strips
Salt and freshly ground pepper
1 medium onion, halved and thinly sliced
4 crusty hero rolls or Italian bread cut into wedges, split

PREPARATION

Place the sausages in a medium skillet with ½ cup water. Cover the skillet and cook over medium heat until the water evaporates and the sausages begin to brown. Uncover and cook, turning the sausages occasionally, until browned on all sides. Remove the sausages to a plate.

Add the oil to the skillet and heat over medium heat. Add the peppers and salt and pepper to taste, cover, and cook, stirring often, until the peppers are softened, about 10 minutes. Add the onion and cook 10 minutes more, until the peppers are tender and lightly browned.

Add the sausages to the pan, with a couple of tablespoons of water. Cover and cook 5 minutes more.

Open the rolls and pull out some of the soft crumb. Stuff the rolls with the sausages, peppers, and onions. Serve hot.

HOT MEATBALL AND MOZZARELLA HEROES

Serves 6

INGREDIENTS

MEATBALLS

1 pound ground beef or a combination of beef and pork

½ cup plain dry bread crumbs, preferably homemade from Italian bread

2 large eggs, beaten

1 teaspoon very finely minced garlic

½ cup freshly grated Pecorino Romano

2 tablespoons finely chopped fresh flat-leaf parsley

1 teaspoon salt

Freshly ground pepper to taste

2 tablespoons olive oil

2½ cups Tomato Sauce (see page 32)

6 crusty hero rolls or Italian bread cut into wedges, split

8 ounces fresh mozzarella, sliced

PREPARATION

Combine all of the meatball ingredients in a large bowl and mix together thoroughly with your hands. Rinse your hands with cool water and lightly shape the mixture into 1½-inch meatballs.

Heat the oil in a large heavy skillet. Add the meatballs and brown them well on all sides. (They will finish cooking later.) Remove the meatballs to a plate.

Bring the sauce to a simmer in a large saucepan or skillet over low heat. Add the meatballs and cook, turning them occasionally, for 10 minutes.

Preheat the broiler. Open the rolls and pull out some of the soft crumb. Add the meatballs and sauce. Place a slice or two of mozzarella on top of the meatballs in each sandwich. Place the open sandwiches on a baking sheet, and run them under the broiler briefly to melt the cheese.

Close the sandwiches and serve immediately.

VEAL AND PEPPER HEROES

Serves 6

INGREDIENTS

¼ cup olive oil

1¼ pounds boneless veal shoulder, trimmed and cut into 3 x 1 x ½-inch strips

Salt and freshly ground pepper

3 large bell peppers and 2 red peppers, cored, seeded, and cut into ½-inch-wide strips

1 large onion, halved and thinly sliced

One 28-ounce can Italian peeled tomatoes, chopped with their juice

½ teaspoon dried oregano

Pinch of crushed red pepper

6 crusty hero rolls, split

PREPARATION

In a large skillet, heat 2 tablespoons of the oil over medium high heat. Add the veal and cook, stirring occasionally, until nicely browned on all sides, about 10 to 12 minutes. Sprinkle with salt and pepper. Remove the veal to a plate.

Pour the remaining 2 tablespoons of oil into the pan and add the peppers. Cover and cook, stirring frequently until the peppers are softened, about 10 minutes.

Add the onions and cook 10 minutes more or until lightly browned. Sprinkle with salt and pepper. Remove the peppers and onions to a plate.

Add the tomatoes, oregano, and crushed red pepper to the pan and stir well. Season to taste with salt. Return the veal to the skillet and bring to a simmer. Turn the heat to low, partially cover the pan, and cook 40 to 45 minutes, or until the meat is fork-tender. If the pan becomes too dry, add a little water.

Stir in the peppers and onions and cook 5 minutes more. Taste for seasoning.

Open the rolls and pull out some of the soft crumb. Stuff the rolls with the veal and peppers. Serve hot.

CARMELA'S NEW JERSEY CHEESECAKE

Serves 12-15

INGREDIENTS

CRUST

1¼ cups graham cracker crumbs
   (about 10 whole graham crackers)

¼ cup sugar

6 tablespoons (¾ stick) unsalted butter,
   melted

FILLING

1½ cups sugar

¼ cup all-purpose flour

Five 8-ounce packages cream cheese,
   at room temperature

1 tablespoon pure vanilla extract

1 teaspoon grated lemon zest

4 large eggs

1 cup sour cream

2 tablespoons fresh lemon juice

PREPARATION

Place a rack in the center of the oven. Preheat the oven to 325°F. Butter the bottom of a 10 x 3-inch springform pan.

To make the crust, in a small bowl, combine the crumbs with the sugar and butter and stir until moistened. Press evenly over bottom of the pan. Bake the crust until golden, about 8 minutes. Set the pan on a rack to cool. Leave the oven on.

To make the filling, in a large mixer bowl, combine the sugar and flour. Add 2 packages of the cream cheese and beat on medium speed until smooth. Add the remaining cream cheese, the vanilla, and lemon zest and beat on low speed until smooth. Add the eggs one at a time, mixing well after each addition. Add the sour cream and lemon juice and beat just until smooth. Don't overbeat the filling, or you will incorporate air, which could cause the

cake to sink when it cools. Spoon the filling into the pan. Bake 1 hour and 15 minutes, or until the cake is set around the edges but there is about 3 inches in the center that is still soft and slightly wobbly.

Place the cake on a wire rack and let cool 1 hour. This cake always cracks, but it tastes great anyway, and it can be topped with fruit when served.

Wrap the cake, still in the pan, in foil and refrigerate at least 8 hours, or overnight. The cake can be refrigerated for up to 3 days before serving.

Remove the cake from the refrigerator about 1 hour before serving. Run a knife around the edge of the cake and remove the sides of the pan.

Chapter 9

ADULT BIRTHDAY PARTIES

he older you get, the more people like to celebrate the fact that you are still around. Every turn of the decade provides an excuse for merrymaking, but for 85 million post-war baby boomers, the Big 5-0 and the Big 6-0 are coming up very quickly. Actually, those of us of a certain age—forty-plus, to be nice about it—are faced with a whole assortment of adult birthdays. Our parents are celebrating seventy through ninety while our friends and spouses are celebrating forty through sixty while our kids are celebrating twenty through forty. If you happen to have grandchildren, that's not such a big obligation for Grandma and Grandpa; you just show up for the snapshots.

Just as there are myriad ways to stage a toddler's birthday, there are many imaginative twists to add to your best friend's fiftieth. If you want to go all out, and the guest list can afford it, you can fly in old friends from grade school on to surprise their aging comrade. This is tantamount to organizing a class reunion. You can, and should, work out cut-rate hotel arrangements and group dining discounts, and maybe rent out a local rec hall or multipurposed room for dancing. This is big-time party plan-

ning and deserves its own guidebook. Thankfully, in the case of my own closest friends and family, pretty much everyone we've ever known lives within a twenty-mile radius of each other. They can all drive to the party. It's almost quaint, isn't it?—like Norman Rockwell with an Italian-American accent.

So my focus here is on the at-home party planned to fit the likes and dislikes of the adult birthday honoree, or guest of honor (GOH). Here's one idea: if it's your own birthday, and you're included in the early planning, think long and hard about not having it in your own home. Even if your spouse promises that you will have absolutely nothing to do, rest assured that you'll have a lot to do. The closer you get to the big day, the more you'll see things that need fixing, brightening, recovering, repainting, and replacing. The night before, you'll have carpenters moving walls or swapping out those dowdy double-hung windows for something French. If you're that kind of domestic perfectionist, which, I confess, I am, ask your best friend to host the affair and avoid the grief. Or go the other direction and use the party as an excuse to redecorate the whole house!

At home or away, I say make the game plan simple. Streamers and balloons always work. Make the menu easy to prepare well ahead of time. If the setting is informal and the mood casual, which I prefer for these kind of friend-fests, talk your spouse—in my case, husband—into cooking on the outdoor grill, even if it is his or her birthday. For many, grilling calms the nerves, especially if all the attention is focused on you. Handled right, it can be like the famous story of Tom Sawyer and whitewashing the picket fence. If others see you having a good time at the grill, they'll soon be begging to do it for you, and you can wander off to tell stories and enjoy your big day.

Besides some delicious food, commemorate the

INVITATIONS

My advice: Make it personal. Use a picture of the GOH as a messy two-year-old, a high school nerd, or a long-haired 60s hippie. Photocopy and then paste on one side of a heavy card with party details on the back. Maybe their whole life can be summed up by that great photo of Richard Nixon with Elvis. Or just Elvis. Or a Vietnam-era peace sign. You could also send out a small box full of fake memorabilia, like a toy soldier (for the vet) or a toy champagne bottle and glass. Go to the dollhouse section of a toy store; you'll be surprise what you might find that fits your GOH to a tee.

You Are Invited...

to Tony's 50th birthday party at our home in North Caldwell
Honoring: Tony Soprano

WHERE: Call for driving directions

WHEN: Saturday, August 6th at 6:00 pm

affair and lead the toasts with something unique and memorable—a fine champagne, a very fine wine, a legendary drink like Prosecco or grappa. This could be a once-in-a-lifetime experience, otherwise known as the Prosecco or Grappa Birthday.

If you want to do something outlandish for a friend or spouse, again think of the person you want most to please, the honoree. For instance, if he or she thinks the super group Cream was the last "real" rock band, hire a live DJ who specializes in music of that era. You can rent a Good Humor truck for the day for the city-raised celebrant, or a cotton candy machine, or even a rock-climbing wall ($1,000 for four hours) for your more adventurous friends. You could anchor the whole event around something as simple as an outdoor film projection system so that everyone can sit on the grass and watch the person of the hour's favorite all-time movie. (I would pick *An Affair to Remember* and make my husband sit through the whole thing.)

Don't go crazy, but think about the one extravagant surprise that would bring a genuine smile to

TONY'S 50th

Using my own husband as an example, here's a list of some surprises he might want at his fiftieth birthday bash.

1 A Dean Martin impersonator.

2 An outdoor screening of his favorite film, *The Public Enemy*, starring James Cagney.

3 You can't go wrong with Cuban cigars or a nice bottle of Dom Perignon, though he has plenty of both around the house.

4 Don't get him a ritzy watch. He has a dozen of them.

5 He loves to play golf, so a monogrammed putter might be appropriate.

6 He once had a beautiful painting made of him and his favorite race horse, but it engendered bad memories. An oil painting of his children would make him cry.

7 Animal lover that he is, I always thought of getting him a cockatoo or an iguana, but animals are very personal and can often backfire as presents. They demand a lot of long-term maintenance. Maybe a pet rabbit, spayed of course, and a year's supply of those little food pellets.

8 *The World At War*, an eleven-volume DVD of the history of World War II from the History Channel. Anything about the Roman Empire would be good too.

the birthday boy or girl. A Dean Martin imperson-ator, for instance, would be great. A Dean Martin impersonator plus a rock-climbing wall could lead to a trip to the ER. Martinis and mountaineering don't mix.

You could also get out the poster board and glue and make a pictorial timeline of the life of the GOH, using as many embarrassing one-too-many photos as available. Mount these along a long wall or two like a gallery show. By the time the guests get to "Second Gallbladder Operation," they'll be ready to cheer on the birthday boy or girl for still walking upright.

A friend of mine who threw a sixtieth dinner party for herself stood up at the end of the evening, went around the room, and said some-thing personal and flattering about every person there. First of all, it was an act of memory that few of us could pull off at sixty, but more importantly, it was an act of kindness and friendship that left everyone feeling like the guest of honor.

Adult birthday parties are not really about pres-ents, are they? They're about longevity and the sweetness of life.

limoncello

Known as *il liquore del sol*–the liqueur of the sun–limoncello is a pale yellow tart-but-sweet liqueur beloved by Italians everywhere. It is made from grain alcohol infused with lemon peel and it is strong–64 proof, 32 percent alcohol.

The name limoncello comes from *limone*, Italian for lemon. Originally a product of the outsized lemons grown along the Amalfi Coast of Southern Italy, it was home brewed from closely guarded family recipes for centuries. Now, like pizza and pesto, it's consumed the world over. Which region of Italy now makes the best limoncello depends on who's talking.

In the United States it costs around $20 to $30 a bottle. Usually drunk cold after dinner, it's kept in the freezer, then served in small chilled shooter glasses and sipped slowly. It can also be poured over ice cream.

BIRTHSTONES

You can arrange the décor of a birthday around a theme as simple and elegant as birthstones and flowers. Pick a month and go from there.

- January: garnet, carnation
- February: amethyst, violet
- March: aquamarine, daffodils
- April: diamond, sweet pea
- May: emerald, lily of the valley
- June: pearl, rose
- July: ruby, larkspur
- August: onyx, gladiola
- September: sapphire, aster
- October: opal, marigold
- November: topaz, chrysanthemum
- December: turquoise, narcissus

WHAT NOT TO DO AT A SENIOR BIRTHDAY
by Hugh De Angelis

This is my father, Hugh De Angelis, a member of "The Greatest Generation," among other things. He insisted on contributing to the book. *CS*

My daughter, Carmela, asked me to contribute some birthday no-no's here because, one, I guess, I don't like birthday parties in general, and two, at my age, I've had more of them than anyone else in this book. My overall feeling is, do what you want—hey, it's your party, not mine—but don't do the following:

1 No age-insulting gag gifts like prune juice, Ensure, adult diapers, Viagra, hair dye, denture cream, expandable pants, or a large-print *New York Times*.

2 Do not make everyone say something nice about the honoree. Some will be tongue-tied; others will say something they think is amusing— like, "Bert is the cheapest so-and-so I've ever known"—which will upset the cheap so-and-so being recognized.

3 No black balloons, black armbands, or cardboard coffins with "RIP" written on the lid, at least not in the Soprano-De Angelis family. Death is too close in our life to laugh about.

4 Don't allow the party givers to disinvite someone you want to invite, even if it's a surprise party and even if the party giver is your wife. She might think the guy is not good enough for your daughter but what do you care? You like him, he actually bought you that gun you wanted, and he should be there.

5 Don't make the birthday person open his or her presents in front of the whole crowd. Do it later when they won't have to be nice.

6 Do get drunk. It's your birthday and you don't have that many left.

PEOPLE HATE SURPRISE PARTIES
by Peter Paul "Paulie Walnuts" Gualtieri

Let's face it, no one likes a surprise party, but hey, people insist on giving them. Naturally, there's a right way and a wrong way to toss one. If the surprisee, as it were, should find out ahead of time, you got egg on your face. How to prevent this? Know who you are telling and tell them only by phone, pay phone if possible, to avoid detection. Don't send any written material that can be discovered or traced. For people who are stupid and/or forgetful, give them false information—different date, different location, that kind of thing—and only tell them the truth a few hours before the real deal. If you're inviting long-lost friends, make sure Birthday Boy doesn't hate their guts or owe them money. It could get messy.

No cars in front of the house, but you already knew that, right?

For the honoree, find someone with an active brain to bring him, and do not come up with a phony excuse to suck him in. Don't tell your eighty-year-old grandpa that you need him to fix your roof on Friday night at nine. Tell him that Friday at nine—a full week before his actual birthday—you want him to come by to regale the kids about the time he almost met Harry Truman. He'll never second-guess you on that one. And make dead sure the person in charge of lying is a good liar. Personally, I know no bad liars among my friends, but your acquaintances might be different. Do not pick the guy with the "I got a secret" face.

One last thing: if it's an old person you're surprising, no screaming or excessive back-patting when the door opens. "The silent killer," i.e., heart failure, could end the festivities right there.

GRILLED BRUSCHETTA

Serves 12

INGREDIENTS

12 thick slices crusty Italian or other chewy, crusty bread

6 large garlic cloves, halved

½ cup extra virgin olive oil

Coarse salt

PREPARATION

Heat a barbecue grill or a large grill pan. Place the bread on the grill or in the pan and cook until golden brown on the first side, about 2 minutes. Turn the bread and brown on the other side.

Remove the bread to a platter. Rub the cut sides of the garlic over one side of each slice of bread. Drizzle generously with oil. Sprinkle with coarse salt. Serve immediately.

CHOPPED SALAD

Serves 6

INGREDIENTS

⅓ cup extra virgin olive oil

2 to 3 tablespoons balsamic vinegar

½ teaspoon dried oregano

Salt and freshly ground pepper

1 pint grape or cherry tomatoes, halved

4 green onions, thinly sliced (about ¾ cup)

2 small cucumbers, chopped into ¾-inch pieces (about 1 heaping cup)

½ small head iceberg lettuce, trimmed, washed, and chopped
   into ¾-inch pieces (about 5 cups)

½ small head escarole, trimmed, washed, and cut into
   bite-sized pieces (about 3 cups)

PREPARATION

In a small jar, combine the oil, vinegar, oregano, and salt and pepper to taste. Shake well. Let stand until ready to use.

In a large salad bowl, combine all of the remaining ingredients. (You can use other vegetables, like radicchio, fennel, radishes, celery, or carrots and whatever else is in season.) Cover and refrigerate up to 3 hours.

When ready to serve, shake the dressing again. Add the dressing to the salad and toss well. Taste for seasoning. Serve immediately.

GRILLED MEATBALL AND SAUSAGE SKEWERS

Serves 8

INGREDIENTS

½ cup plain dry bread crumbs, preferably homemade from Italian bread

½ cup water

1 pound ground beef sirloin

½ cup freshly grated Parmigiano-Reggiano or Pecorino Romano

¼ cup chopped fresh flat-leaf parsley

1 large egg, lightly beaten

1 large garlic clove, finely chopped

1 teaspoon salt

Freshly ground pepper

2 medium red onions, each cut into 8 wedges

16 bay leaves

1 pound hot or sweet Italian-style pork sausages, cut into 1-inch pieces

PREPARATION

Soak 8 long bamboo skewers in water for 30 minutes.

In a large bowl, soak the bread crumbs in the water until the liquid is absorbed.

Add the beef, cheese, parsley, egg, garlic, salt, and pepper to taste. Mix well. Moisten your hands and shape the mixture into 1½-inch meatballs. (Don't make them larger, or they will break apart on the skewers.)

Alternate the onions, meatballs, bay leaves, and sausage pieces on the skewers. Cover and chill 30 minutes to allow the meatball mixture to firm up.

Place the grill rack or broiler pan 4 inches from the heat. Prepare a medium-hot charcoal fire or preheat a gas grill or the broiler.

Brush the grill rack with oil. Place the skewers on the grill or the broiler pan and let brown on one side, about 6 minutes. Very carefully turn the skewers and grill until the meat is nicely browned and cooked through, about 5 minutes more.

Serve hot.

BOW TIES WITH FRESH TOMATOES AND MOZZARELLA

Serves 4 to 6

INGREDIENTS

4 ripe medium tomatoes, preferably New Jersey beefsteaks, chopped

½ cup torn fresh basil leaves

⅓ cup extra virgin olive oil

1 garlic clove, finely chopped

Salt and freshly ground pepper

1 pound bow ties (farfalle)

8 ounces fresh mozzarella, cut into small dice

PREPARATION

In a large pasta serving bowl, combine the tomatoes, basil, oil, garlic, and salt and pepper to taste. Let stand at room temperature up to 2 hours.

Bring at least 4 quarts of salted water to a boil in a large pot. Add the pasta, stir well, and cook over high heat, stirring frequently, until the pasta is al dente, tender yet firm to the bite.

Drain the pasta and toss it with the sauce. Add the mozzarella and toss again.

Serve immediately.

PEPPERED PORK TENDERLOINS

Serves 6 to 8

INGREDIENTS

2 tablespoons olive oil

1 tablespoon Dijon mustard

2 teaspoons chopped fresh rosemary

1 teaspoon salt

2 pork tenderloins (about 2 pounds), trimmed and each tied like a roast
   to even the thickness

1 tablespoon coarsely cracked black pepper

PREPARATION

In a small bowl, stir together the oil, mustard, rosemary, and salt. Brush the mixture over the pork. Sprinkle the tenderloins on all sides with the pepper. Cover and refrigerate until ready to cook, up to 4 hours.

Place the grill rack or broiler pan 4 inches from the heat. Prepare a medium-hot charcoal fire or preheat a gas grill or the broiler.

Grill or broil the pork, turning it with tongs so that it is browned on all sides and the meat feels springy when pressed, about 15 to 20 minutes, according to the thickness. The pork should be pink and juicy when cut and an instant-read thermometer inserted in the center should read 150° to 155°F; do not overcook. Transfer the pork to a cutting board and cover with foil. The temperature will continue to rise 5 to 10 degrees as the meat rests. Let stand about 5 minutes.

Remove the strings and carve the pork into ½-inch-thick diagonal slices. Fan them on a serving platter. Serve warm or at room temperature.

GOOGOOTZ GIAMBOTTA

Zucchini Stew

Serves 6

INGREDIENTS

2 medium onions, chopped

3 tablespoons olive oil

1 garlic clove, very finely chopped

6 plum tomatoes, cut into bite-sized pieces

4 medium zucchini, trimmed and cut into bite-sized pieces

2 medium potatoes, peeled and cut into bite-sized pieces

Salt and freshly ground pepper

2 tablespoons chopped fresh basil

PREPARATION

In a large saucepan, cook the onions in the oil over medium heat until softened, about 5 minutes. Stir in the garlic and cook 1 minute more.

Add the tomatoes, zucchini, potatoes, and salt and pepper to taste. Cover and cook over low heat 30 minutes, stirring occasionally, or until the potatoes are very tender. Add a little water if the mixture seems dry.

Remove from the heat and stir in the basil. Serve hot or at room temperature.

QUARESIMALI

Cinnamon Nut Biscotti

Makes about 10 dozen

INGREDIENTS

2 cups all-purpose flour

1¼ cups sugar

1¼ teaspoons ground cinnamon

1 teaspoon baking powder

¼ teaspoon salt

3 large eggs

5 drops cinnamon oil (optional but good; you can buy this in many
   gourmet shops)

1½ cups toasted almonds

1½ cups skinned toasted hazelnuts

PREPARATION

Preheat the oven to 350°F. Butter and flour two large baking sheets. In a large mixing bowl, stir together the flour, sugar, cinnamon, baking powder, and salt.

Beat the eggs with the cinnamon oil, if using. Stir the eggs into the dry ingredients until well blended. Stir in the nuts.

Divide the dough into 6 portions. Moisten your hands with cool water. Shape one portion of the dough into a log about 1½ inches in diameter. Place the log on a prepared baking sheet. Repeat with the remaining dough, spacing the logs about 2 inches apart. (They will spread as they bake.)

Bake 20 to 22 minutes, or until the logs are firm when lightly pressed in the center and lightly browned around the edges.

Remove the logs to a cutting board, but leave the oven on. With a heavy chef's knife, cut the logs diagonally into ½-inch slices.

Place the slices back on the baking sheets and bake until crisp and golden brown, about 10 minutes. Cool the cookies on wire racks.

Store in an airtight container.

LEMON ICE

Serves 10 to 12

INGREDIENTS

1 cup water

1⅓ cups sugar

5 cups ice cubes

1 teaspoon grated lemon zest

1 cup fresh lemon juice

PREPARATION

In a small saucepan over medium heat, bring the water and sugar to a simmer. Cook, stirring occasionally, until the sugar is dissolved, about 3 minutes. Remove from the heat.

Place the ice cubes in a large bowl. Add the sugar syrup and stir until the ice is melted. Stir in the lemon zest and juice. Refrigerate until chilled, about 1 hour.

Freeze the mixture in an ice cream maker following the manufacturer's directions. Or freeze it in a pan, then break it into chunks and puree it in a food processor.

Serve immediately, or scrape the lemon ice into a plastic container, cover, and store in the freezer up to 24 hours. If it gets too hard, let it soften briefly at room temperature.

$\mathcal{T}$HE FINAL CELEBRATION

$\mathcal{I}$t is not my intent to end this book about the joys of entertaining on a down or depressing note, but a) we all pass on, and b) a thoughtful gathering to celebrate the life of a loved one is both a fitting way to end his or her time on earth and a fitting way to end a survey of family traditions that started with birth. A dear one's passing is always bittersweet. We are deeply saddened by their absence but are equally heartened by the nostalgic pull of old memories; even the painful ones have now lost their sting. It's almost an obligation to the deceased to stage a post-funeral buffet that honors his or her life. Certainly none of us would like our funeral to end with punch and cookies in the church foyer or take-out food from Chicken All Day. We'd want something more representative of who we were, how we lived, and what we ate. The buffet, in other words, is an extension of the loved one who cannot attend.

In the Catholic tradition, the post-funeral buffet is called the Mercy Dinner. It immediately follows the service, and the priest in charge often extends an invitation to the congregation at the end of the service. The Mercy Dinner is usually held at a relative's home, a hall at the church, or in a reserved space in the back of a restaurant. If the location is the church hall, you usually pay a fee and the Ladies' Guild of the parish acts as the caterer; they fix the meal, serve, and clean up. I, for one, prefer the at-home buffet. The setting is more intimate and more comfortable and the goings-on, including the food, more personal.

No matter your religious bent, there are a few matters to consider in arranging a buffet in your home. First of all, the menu should in some way reflect or even illuminate the deceased. If he or she was an older person born abroad, for instance, some hint of their native fare should be included. If they were born Swedish, for instance, the buffet might include Swedish meatballs, flatbread, or maybe even the traditional Swedish drink, aquavit. Being Italian and being, in general, a very food-oriented people, both old and young in our general circle like much of the same food. The menu I've chosen for this chapter, however, points to dishes that an older Italian-American might feel especially deeply about.

UNCLE JUNIOR ON WAKES

Earlier, I interviewed Uncle Junior Soprano on his childhood Christmas and that went so well, I thought I'd introduce him one last time on the subject of wakes. Given both his advanced age and his straightforward, no-nonsense manner, I thought he could help us appreciate the true meaning of a final celebration. *CS*

JUNIOR: Again? You have more questions?
CARMELA: Now we're talking about wakes and their meaning. . . .
JUNIOR: My brother Johnny's wake was the saddest day of my life. People were nice. They brought food 'cause my mother was a crappy cook, but I ate nothing. My father couldn't string two sentences together, so Old Man DiMeo got up and gave a great speech about how Johnny was the best and brightest in all of West Orange, if not farther, and how he loved him like a son, and who was going to take his place? That's when I left the room. I went upstairs and cried like a baby.
CARMELA: You have no happy remembrances of that day?
JUNIOR: None. There were a few flowers from the garden, that's all. People gave my dad money to pay for the funeral. He drank it up in no time. Next question.
CARMELA: Have you thought about dying, Uncle Jun'?
JUNIOR: What do you think? I'm closing in on eighty, barely leave the house, and can't remember what I had for break-fast. Yes, I hope it's nice and peaceful. I look forward to run-ning into Johnny.
CARMELA: You aren't afraid of dying?
JUNIOR: What's to be afraid of? Even if it hurts, it's not going to hurt for long. And I'm not worried about hell, if that's what you're worried about. Hell is for Hitler and the Oklahoma City bomber, the little creep. I just did what I had to do.
CARMELA: If you could plan your own wake, what would you specify?
JUNIOR: No harsh or sarcastic words from my brother's son, to start with. No jokes about my way with women, should that come up. I'd like only the old music to be played, sad old bal-lads to be sung live, if you can find some-one to sing them. Maybe I should record a few just in case. How's that?
CARMELA: That's a wonderful idea. AJ can burn a CD.
JUNIOR: I said "record," not destroy. And I want the food I can no longer eat without getting gastric dis-tress. Peppers, gar-lic, onions, cream puffs, you name it. And none of that crap that passes for "Italian" down at the grocery, like, you know, flavored bread crumbs, marinara in a jar, Italian sausage from Arkansas. I crushed one of those underfoot once, just to make my point.
CARMELA: Please, Uncle Junior, I would never. . .
JUNIOR: And the only wine served should be the homemade wine the Bucassi brothers used to make. . . Boy, did that swill get you. . .
CARMELA: The Bucassi brothers died in 1963.
JUNIOR (not listening): Okay, to review, a lot of food, no crap, a lot of Bucassi vino, a nice speech from Bacala, since he was always the nicest to me of all those bums, and me singing like Caruso on the Victrola. I think that about does it. (Gets up.) I'm taking a nap.
CARMELA: Thank you, Uncle Junior, and God bless.

There is no "decoration" that's appropriate for this event except, perhaps, to use your best china, stemware, and table linens, or even rent them if necessary. Paper plates and cups seem a little too casual for such a solemn gathering, at least to my mind. The main item of décor will probably be flowers, either brought from church or sent directly to the home. Flowers normally sent to the church or funeral home fall into two categories: floral arrangements, in baskets or vases, and sprays, designed to be seen from one side only, often on easels, and often in shapes like wreaths, crosses, hearts, or horseshoes. Typically only floral arrangements are sent to the residence or brought from the service. It would be hard to have a gathering at your home with people having to sidestep a forest of often-oversized and ungainly sprays. Leave them at the church and ask that they be passed on to someone who needs them.

People will send you the flowers they will send you, and that's fine, but if you're confused about what *you* should send to a funeral or wake, here are the safe bets: white roses, white chrysanthemums, lilies, and carnations are traditional funeral flowers. Of course, priority should be given to a flower especially reminiscent of the deceased, but that's a judgment call only you can make.

Two other touches are appropriate for a wake and buffet: photos and a guest book. Depending on your taste, you can arrange photos of the deceased around the room or group them on a photo board or in a scrapbook. Often one photo alone will tell a compelling story, especially if it is a young photo of an older person, say, an immigrant just getting off the boat in the 1920s or 30s. Most of the people in the room only know that person from, say, age fifty on. Learning about the person at twenty can start a whole other conversation. You could write and print up a short biography, another gift for the young.

ON YOUR TOMBSTONE

What would you like written on your tombstone or marker? Interesting question, isn't it? Here are some of the fascinating answers I collected. *CS*

PAULIE WALNUTS: Very easy. "He was nice to his mother and always well groomed."

AJ SOPRANO: "Rock on!"

ROSALIE APRILE: "God, please take me to my two Jackies in heaven."

JANICE SOPRANO: I plan to be cremated, taken to a distant sandy beach, and have my ashes merged with the out flowing tide. If there is some kind of memorial plaque, it should be inscribed with a poem of my own writing, composed within days of my demise, to keep it fresh and in the moment.

CHRISTOPHER MOLTISANTI: I've thought a lot about this and have arrived at one of two choices. "He beat drugs and lived a good life." Or, "What does it profit a man if he has money but no friends?" Both will give the sightseers something to think about.

DR. JENNIFER MELFI: Hmm, I don't know. Does there have to be something besides your name? I think I'd like "Jennifer Melfi, Mother, Doctor, Friend." Or maybe just "Jennifer Melfi, M.D." But that sounds like a résumé, doesn't it?

SILVIO DANTE: "This is the life that I chose. Happily."

OUT-OF-TOWN GUESTS

Dealing with out-of-town guests in your home can be a hassle, but if that is the only option, prepare in a way that will make you both comfortable. If you have to stick a roll-away or a futon in a den or office, hide the sleeping space with a decorative screen of some kind. Also, designate some closet space nearby for the guest and have a few extra hangers in there. If you have a guest room, all the better. In either case, try to accommodate your guest by thinking about what you'd like to have around if you were visiting someone else. Here's a short list of items I'd include:

- A portable TV or radio, especially in a guest room. Like everyone else, guests like to get away from the crowd and watch the eleven o'clock news.

- An alarm clock, a carafe and glass for water, even a little nightstand tray to put things like wallets, keys, and earrings.

- A basket of food to snack on: crackers, nuts, fruits, chocolates, i.e., all those things they charge you a fortune for in a hotel mini-bar. (Even if your guest is staying in a hotel room, make up this basket and get it there before they arrive.)

- A reading light, for sure, and maybe even a scented candle, but not too close to the bedding.

- Along with fresh towels for the guest, maybe a guest bathrobe, which they will love, or a small basket full of hotel-sized toiletries like a mini bottle of shaving cream, a razor, shampoo, toothpaste, and mouthwash. "Borrow" them on your next hotel visit and recycle them at home.

MUSIC ♪

Assuming you don't have someone like Junior singing live, Italian opera is always good, at least in my family. Here are some of my favorite recordings.

- *Tosca*, Maria Callas, Giuseppe di Stefano, et al.
- *La Traviata*, Maria Callas, Orchestra e Coro del Teatro alla Scala, et al.
- *Turandot*, Bonaldo Giaiotti, Guido Mazzini, et al.
- *Madama Butterfly*, Angelo Mercuriali, Carol Bergonzi, et al.

A guest book full of short inscriptions and remembrances can be something you read to your grandchildren some day. You can buy guest books at a stationery store, in any design or shape you want. I prefer one with unlined pages as a way to nudge mourners to write more than just their name and "He was a good soul." In fact, you and others in the family should fill out the first few pages with enough memories to encourage others to follow suit. Remember, you might see Grandma in one way while her friend of fifty years may have a completely different take. Even if some people speak at either the service or the wake, a common practice these days, most will not. Personally, I think it's awful to force people to speak at a wake, especially if they are asked to bend the truth and say something nice and gushy about a not-so-nice person. The guest book is a safe way for both the shy and the double-minded to say what they want or say nothing at all.

One last thing: though still quite customary, wearing black to a funeral or wake is not absolutely necessary. As times change, all-black has gone the way of the widow's veil and the funeral walk. Tasteful and modest, no matter the color, will fit right in with black and somber. Nothing flashy, of course. Of all the events in this book, someone else's funeral is not about you.

PASTA PISELLI

Pasta Pezeel ❦ Pasta with Peas and Eggs

Serves 6

INGREDIENTS

2 medium onions, chopped

¼ cup olive oil

2 cups fresh peas or one 10-ounce package frozen peas, partially thawed

Salt and freshly ground pepper

1 pound small elbows or ditalini

3 large eggs

½ cup freshly grated Pecorino Romano

½ cup torn fresh basil or flat-leaf parsley leaves

PREPARATION

In a large saucepan, cook the onions in the oil over medium heat until tender and golden, about 10 minutes. Add the peas and salt and pepper to taste. Cook 5 minutes, or until the peas are tender. Remove from heat.

Meanwhile, bring 4 quarts of salted water to boil in a large pot. Add the pasta and cook, stirring often, until the pasta is al dente, tender yet still firm to the bite.

Beat the eggs, cheese, and salt and pepper to taste in a small bowl until blended.

Drain the pasta, reserving ½ cup of the cooking water. Add the pasta to the pan with the peas and cook over medium heat. Stirring constantly, add the egg and cheese mixture, and cook about 2 minutes, or until the eggs are lightly set. Add a little of the cooking water if the pasta seems dry. Stir in the basil. Serve hot.

GNOCCHI

Serves 6 to 8

INGREDIENTS

2 pounds baking potatoes, scrubbed

2 large egg yolks, beaten

2 teaspoons salt

About 2½ cups all-purpose flour

Meat Sauce (page 82) or Tomato Sauce (page 32)

½ cup freshly grated Pecorino Romano
or Parmigiano-Reggiano

PREPARATION

Put the potatoes in a large pot with cold water to cover; cover and bring to a boil. Cook 20 minutes, or until the potatoes are tender. Drain and let the potatoes cool slightly.

While the potatoes are still warm, peel them and cut into chunks. Finely mash the potatoes with a potato masher or pass through a ricer or food mill into a medium bowl. (Do not use a food processor, or they will become gluey.) Add the egg yolks and salt. Stir in 1½ cups of the flour just until blended.

Scrape the potatoes onto a floured surface. Knead briefly, adding more flour as necessary to make a soft, slightly sticky dough. The dough should be stiff enough so that the gnocchi will hold their shape when cooked but not so much that they become tough. (Test the dough by bringing a small saucepan of salted water to a boil. Pinch off a small piece of the dough about the size of a grape and cook until it rises to the surface, then about 30 seconds more. Scoop out the gnocchi and taste. If it is mushy, knead in a little additional flour.)

Set the dough aside for a moment. Scrape the board to remove scraps of dough. Wash and dry your hands.

Sprinkle two large baking sheets with flour. Cut the dough into 8 pieces. Keeping the remaining dough

covered, roll one piece into a long rope about ¾ inch thick. Cut the rope into ½-inch pieces. Hold a fork in one hand with the tines pointed down. With the thumb of the other hand, roll each piece of dough over the back of the tines, pressing lightly to make ridges on one side and an indentation from your finger on the other. Drop the gnocchi onto one of the baking sheets. Repeat with the remaining dough.

Cover the gnocchi loosely with a towel or aluminum foil and refrigerate until ready to cook, or overnight. (The gnocchi can also be frozen. Place the baking sheets in the freezer for 1 hour, or until the gnocchi are firm. Put the gnocchi in a plastic bag. Freeze up to 1 month. Do not thaw before cooking.)

Bring a large pot of salted water to a boil. Lower the heat so that the water boils gently. Add a spoonful of the sauce to a large heated serving bowl.

Drop about half of the gnocchi into the water. Stir gently to separate the pieces. Cook for 30 seconds after the gnocchi rise to the surface. Skim the gnocchi from the pot with a sieve, draining them well, and transfer to the bowl. Spoon on more of the sauce and stir gently. Cook and drain the remaining gnocchi in the same way, and add them to the bowl with the remaining sauce.

Sprinkle with the cheese. Serve hot.

PASTA E CECI

Pasta Cheech ❖ *Pasta and Chickpeas*

Serves 4 to 6

INGREDIENTS

2 ounces pancetta, chopped

¼ cup olive oil

3 garlic cloves, finely chopped

Pinch of crushed red pepper

Two 16-ounce cans chickpeas, drained

Salt

2 cups chopped canned tomatoes

¼ cup chopped fresh flat-leaf parsley

8 ounces spaghetti, broken into bite-sized pieces

Coarsely ground black pepper

PREPARATION

In a large pot, cook the pancetta in the oil over medium heat until lightly browned, about 10 minutes. Add the garlic and crushed red pepper and cook until the garlic is golden.

Add the chickpeas, tomatoes, and parsley, bring to a simmer, and cook 15 minutes. Crush some of the chickpeas with the back of a spoon.

Add 4 cups water to the pot and bring to a simmer. Add the pasta and salt to taste. Cook, stirring frequently, until the pasta is al dente, tender yet still firm to the bite. Add more water if necessary to prevent the pasta from sticking to the bottom of the pot. The consistency should be just loose enough to require eating with a spoon.

Let cool slightly before serving. Serve with coarsely ground black pepper.

ROAST PORK LOIN

Serves 8

INGREDIENTS

4 large garlic cloves
2 tablespoons chopped fresh rosemary
Salt and freshly ground pepper
1 bone-in center-cut pork rib roast (about 4 pounds)
2 tablespoons olive oil

PREPARATION

Preheat the oven to 325°F.

Very finely chop the garlic and rosemary together. Place the mixture in a small bowl, add salt and pepper to taste, and mix well.

Place the roast fat side up in the pan. With a small knife, make 1-inch-deep slits all over the surface of the pork. Stuff a little of the garlic mixture into each slit. Rub the roast all over with the olive oil.

Roast 1½ hours, or until the center of the meat reaches 150°F on an instant-read thermometer. The exact time depends on how thick the meat is. Transfer the meat to a cutting board. Cover with foil to keep warm and let rest 10 minutes before slicing.

Slice the pork and arrange it on a warm serving platter. Spoon the vegetables around the meat. Serve hot.

BROCCOLI RABE WITH GARLIC AND HOT PEPPER

Serves 8

INGREDIENTS

4 large garlic cloves, thinly sliced

Pinch of crushed red pepper

¼ cup olive oil

2 bunches (about 1 pound each) broccoli rabe, trimmed and cut
    into 2-inch pieces

Salt

PREPARATION

In a large skillet, cook the garlic and crushed red pepper in the oil over medium heat until the garlic is golden, about 2 minutes.

Add the broccoli rabe, ¼ cup water, and salt to taste. Cover the pan and cook until the broccoli rabe is tender, about 5 minutes. If the pan becomes too dry, add a little more water.

Serve hot or at room temperature. This is also good tossed with hot cooked pasta.

PATATE ALLA PIZZAIOLA

Potatoes Pizzaiol' ❀ Pizza-Style Potatoes

Serves 6

INGREDIENTS

2 pounds potatoes, peeled and cut into wedges

6 large plum tomatoes, cut into thin wedges

2 medium onions, sliced

1 garlic clove, finely chopped

½ teaspoon dried oregano

¼ cup olive oil

Salt and freshly ground pepper

¼ cup freshly grated Pecorino Romano

PREPARATION

Preheat the oven to 450°F.

In a roasting pan large enough to hold all the ingredients in a single layer, toss together the potatoes, tomatoes, onions, garlic, oregano, oil, and salt and pepper to taste. Spread the vegetables out evenly in the pan.

Roast the vegetables, stirring 2 or 3 times, for 1 hour, or until the potatoes are cooked through. Sprinkle with the cheese and cook 5 minutes more.

Serve hot.

CREAM PUFFS

Makes 1 dozen

INGREDIENTS

1 cup water

8 tablespoons (1 stick) unsalted butter

½ teaspoon salt

1 cup all-purpose flour

4 large eggs, at room temperature

FILLING

Ricotta Cream (page 127) or your
   favorite ice cream

Confectioners' sugar

PREPARATION

Preheat the oven to 400°F. Butter and flour a large baking sheet.

Put the water, butter, and salt in a medium saucepan and bring to a boil over medium-low heat. Remove from the heat. Add the flour all at once and stir well with a wooden spoon until the flour is completely mixed in. Return the saucepan to medium heat and cook, stirring constantly and turning the dough often, until the dough begins to leave a thin film on the bottom of the saucepan, about 3 minutes. (This dries the dough so the cream puffs will be crisp.) With a rubber spatula, scrape the dough into a large bowl.

With an electric mixer or a wooden spoon, beat in the eggs one at a time until thoroughly blended. Continue to beat until smooth and shiny, about 2 minutes more.

Scoop up a rounded tablespoon of the dough, and use a second spoon to push the dough off the spoon onto

the prepared baking sheet. Repeat to form 12 mounds spaced about 3 inches apart. With moistened fingertips, pat the tops to round the shape.

Bake the cream puffs 40 to 45 minutes, until golden brown. Turn off the oven and remove the puffs. With a small knife, make a small hole in the side of each puff to allow the steam to escape. Return the puffs to the oven for 10 minutes to dry.

Using a serrated knife, cut the puffs crosswise partway in half. Open like a book and scoop out the soft dough from the inside. Transfer to a wire rack and let cool completely.

Spoon the cream into the puffs. Refrigerate up to 3 hours, or serve immediately, dusted with confectioners' sugar. If using ice cream, fill the puffs and serve immediately, or fill and freeze until ready to serve.

PEACHES IN RED WINE

Serves 6

INGREDIENTS

½ cup sugar, or to taste

2½ cups fruity red wine, preferably homemade

6 ripe white or yellow peaches

PREPARATION

In a medium bowl, combine the sugar and wine and stir until sugar is dissolved.

Cut the peaches in half and remove the pits (peeling is optional). Cut the peaches into slices. Stir them into the wine. Cover and let stand 2 to 3 hours.

Spoon the peaches and wine into wineglasses and serve.

AFTERWORD

Well, that's the end of our entertaining journey together. I hope you learned a little about Italian-American food and life and picked up a tidbit here and there to add a dash to your next social occasion, big or small. There were times when I was compiling this book and consulting with family and friends about the broad and almost bottomless topic of entertaining when I would stop and ask myself, "Who really has time for all of this stuff? Will all these tips about napkin folding and charger plates overwhelm the reader? Will they think they'll have to leave town if the salad dish on their buffet table is situated *after* the main entrée? Or if, God forbid, they serve a hearty red wine with fish?"

Of course not. This isn't a test. You don't get a grade for organizing your forks in the right order. But planning a menu and setting a table in a delightful way for a party of twelve is no more "work" than gardening or owning a pleasure boat, if you just take the leap. And feeling that you know both common practices and a few alternatives will make it that much more engaging. You're actually staging an event and entertaining *yourself*. Which is the bottom line—if you aren't having fun planning and hosting a confirmation party, a wedding shower, or a lunch with the girls, your guests probably won't have that much fun either. No one is sticking a gun to your head. If you don't want to go to the trouble, don't.

But, my guess is, you do want to go to the trouble, or at least some trouble, to draw people together. After all, what's closer to a celebration of life than *celebrations?* Look for them, jump into them, charger plates and all, and have a ball. A ball of your own making.

Salut'!

INDEX OF RECIPES

ALLEN RUCKER is the author of five books of nonfiction and humor, including the *New York Times* #1 bestselling *The Sopranos Family Cookbook, The Sopranos: A Family History,* and, with Martin Mull, *The History of White People in America*. His memoir, *Between FDR and Perfect: Life after Paralysis,* will be published in Fall 2006. He lives in Los Angeles.

MICHELE SCICOLONE is the author of numerous Italian cookbooks and teaches cooking classes around the country. Her most recent book is *1,000 Italian Recipes,* published by Wiley. She writes frequently for major food and wine magazines including *Gourmet, Bon Appétit,* and *Wine Spectator.* She grew up in Bensonhurst, Brooklyn, and all of her grandparents come from the Naples area, not far from the Soprano family.